Winning the Battle Against Domestic Violence

"Starting With You"

A self-help and recovery guide written for women seeking to combat the devastating effects of domestic violence. An engaging true-life story filled with practical suggestions and spiritual insight.

by
VIVIEN ROSE

First publication IGNITE PUBLISHING HOUSE

Second publication INGENE PUBLICATIONS

Copyright ©2013 – Vivien Rose

©2013, IGNITE Publishing House 2013

Email: ignitepublishinghouse@gmail.com

All rights reserved. This book is protected under the copyright of the United Kingdom. The use of short quotations or occasional page copying for personal use or groups is permitted and encouraged. It may not be copied or reprinted for profits sake either by an individual or company without the knowledge of the Author or Publisher. Permission will be granted upon request.

Scripture taken from the New King James Version ©1979 by Thomas Nelson, Inc. Used by permission. All rights reserved.

Marketed and Distributed by:
IGNITE Publishing House
Agincourt Road,
Hampstead NW3
London

You can purchase further copies of this book online and future material by the same author from:

www.ignitebenevolencefund.org

Dedication

I dedicate this book to women everywhere who are suffering in silence.

Also I dedicate this book to the glory and honour of my Lord and Saviour, Jesus Christ, who has been faithful to preserve me and bring me safely through the darkest of times – turning my mourning into dancing.

Preface

Why Suffer? Why Pain?

My journey in life
Has been twists and turns,
Highs and lows; Crashes and burns
Yet with tenacity and through tears of pain,
I kept getting up – again and again.

The tests got harder,
The road got steeper,
I often wondered – can I dig any deeper?
No strength left, nothing in reserve
My dreams before me
Were becoming blurred.

In desperation, I called on the Name
Of the Holy One Eternal
And with mercy, He came
Using words of wisdom, love and grace
He mentored my progress,
He coached my pace

Bitter trials endured
Now turned to a college,
Precious lessons of life
Giving me knowledge
Rather than surrender to tactics of blame
I pooled my experience
And I bettered my game.

Why suffer? Why Pain?
Many ask today
The best we can do
Is the hand we play
Faced with turmoil,
Trouble and grief
Let our scars and wounds
Bring others relief

By Vivien Rose

Acknowledgements

For the sake of anonymity, I have not mentioned names, but I wish to thank all those involved in helping me to write, edit and publish this book, especially the team at Ingene Publications. Undoubtedly, the topic is controversial in nature; therefore I sincerely thank my children and family for permitting me to share my experiences so candidly. I am grateful to all the men and women, elders and pastors who counseled and prayed for us. Also special thanks go to my friends for giving me your shoulders to cry on and all your support over the years. You've been true sisters! May you all be richly rewarded for your generosity of heart and spirit. My deepest gratitude goes to the Author and Finisher of my faith, who sustained me through the deep waters of distress, My Shield, My Glory and the One Who lifts up my head.

Contents

Dedication — iii
Foreword — iv
Acknowledgements — vi
Introduction — 1
Chapters

You Are Invaluable	2
No Excuses!	X
Take Cover … Quickly!	XX
Recognising an Abusive Mindset	XX
The Natural, Hurtful and Helpful Response	XX
My Story	XX
Walking Out – The Practicalities	XX
The Road to Recovery	XX
Watch Out For The Potholes	XX
For Bitter or For Better?	XX
Three Stages to Forgiveness	XX
Conclusion	XX

INTRODUCTION

In writing this book, I primarily seek to help women who are experiencing or recovering from domestic violence and abuse within their marriage or relationships.

Though this book is directed at women, I am well aware that many men also suffer from domestic violence and abuse, which has become an increasing concern. To men I say, you are welcome to read this book and I trust you will find principles that will help in your situation. However, I do not assume that all issues pertaining to men and women are necessarily the same.

My intention is to provide practical solutions that will spur you into action and give you the courage to break the cycle of abuse.

This book is written in the context of my own personal experience. You will read excerpts from my fourteen year journey to freedom as I share the various lessons I learned and applied in a transparent, candid and thought-provoking way.

The main message for those that read this book is *"there is hope for you and your entire family but the catch is, you must first save your life before you can save your home"*. There are people out there like me who have suffered through a marriage or relationship crippled by domestic abuse, yet have managed to come out on the other side. You can too.

Today my life is free from domestic abuse, filled with purpose and fulfilment. Despite the setbacks and trials of the past, I have healed. The memories are there, but the pain is gone. Life is good. Above all, I am at peace!

CHAPTER 1

You Are Invaluable

You are invaluable! Read that again, and this time put your name in the sentence. Say it out loud **"I *(say your name)* am invaluable!"**

Your success in overcoming domestic violence and abuse ultimately hinges on your capacity to actually believe *in your infinite* worth as a human being and as a woman. Once you can accept, you are not *less* in any way shape or form – but you are good enough and deserving enough to expect your dignity to be upheld and appreciated – then you will increase your chances of getting free and staying far away from the evil clutches of abuse.

After many years of experiencing pain and heartache in my marriage, I came to the point when I realised that I had to stand up for *me*. I couldn't afford to wait for him to have a change of heart before he would stop hurting me. I had to be the one to take responsibility for my future and that of my children.

Other people could sympathise, counsel, encourage and offer their support. But ultimately, the buck stopped with me. I had to make the hard choices. I knew the things we were suffering behind closed doors, things that are often difficult to articulate or explain. Therefore, I had to believe in better for myself, pray for myself and have faith enough to face the daunting task of obtaining a future for myself and my two children. This meant, plucking up the courage to fight for our dignity, value and worth as human beings *whether* he changed or not.

From a Christian perspective, I believe that every person is born equal in the site of God; uniquely designed and gifted for a special purpose and destiny.

But frankly, irrespective of what your world view may be, it is vitally important you begin to dissect and analyse the way you see yourself and your behavioural responses.

When you suffer any form of abuse, you often come to a place where your esteem is so battered and bruised that you literally lose sight of one very important truth – that is – *You* are irreplaceable.

You don't come from a manufacturing line where they are several others exactly like you waiting to packaged and sold. You are not a consumable product which people use and throw away. The secret ingredient to your life cannot simply be bottled, trademarked or duplicated at will. Think about it, there has never been anyone on the planet like you, nor will there ever be again. That makes you acutely precious. What's more, you are priceless and irreplaceable!

Yet the insidious nature of domestic abuse is such that when we have been consistently maltreated and insulted we start making excuses for the aggressor to ourselves. Deep down, we gradually convince ourselves that somehow we deserve it. After all, if only we were X, Y or Z, things would improve right? What a lie.

After several years of talking, arguing and pleading with my husband, I learnt this lesson the hard way. It became blatantly clear that if I didn't send out the message *'enough is enough'* the pattern of abuse would not stop.

Even though, there were good months and bad months, no lasting change happened until I began to respect myself *as an individual.*

Yes that's right – the typical response is: we must think of others first but this is like putting the cart before the horse. The correct thing to do is to respect yourself as an individual *first* because the measure of self respect we walk in is the gauge others use in dealing with us as people.

Unwittingly in our subconscious, we value our status as wives or our family, our careers and our reputation *more* than our worth as individuals. We worry about what people will say or do and we over-stress on the traditions of our culture, desperately trying to avoid disrupting our daily lives. Subsequently, we remain silent.

In an effort to safeguard the status-quo, we inadvertently place the acceptance and opinions of others above our own security. Sadly, this means, we remain in bondage to the abuse. Worse still, we continue to endure untold suffering while the nightmare continues, the atrocities to our dignity escalate and our relationship deteriorates.

If this is a picture of what you are experiencing, I can only implore you to remember that your life as an individual really does count. When you look at your life through the divine lens; a person of infinite worth, beloved creation of God, made in His image for hope and purpose; then you will begin to make decisions that line up with your true identity.

> ***Psalm 139:13*** *"For you formed my inward parts; You covered me in my mother's womb."*
>
> ***Psalm 139:14*** *"I will praise You, for I am fearfully and wonderfully made."*
>
> ***Psalm 139:17-18*** *"How precious are Your thoughts to me O God! How great is the sum*

> *of them! If I should count them, they would be more in number than the sand."*

Psalm 139 is a wonderful account of how God took His time and care in making us. It goes on to talk of how He still thinks about us constantly, wishing us success, planning for our good!

Surely the whole point of the crucifixion was Christ's way of showing us how committed he was to buy back our right to an abundant life, here on earth and in heaven. He wants us to enjoy a life filled with love, liberty and peace forever! Its precisely for this reason that I chose to resist the abuse which threatened this hope.

> ***1 Corinthians 7:23*** *"You were bought at a price; do not become slaves of men."*

When the revelation of these words begins to seep into your subconscious mind you are literally repairing your self worth. Without realising it, you are fortifying those inner places of confidence that have been dented and distorted out of shape by the barrage of physical, emotional and psychological wounds inflicted on you by your loved one.

The realisation alone, that God the Creator of the Universe, the One who has the power to give and take life, actually respects and values your personhood beyond measure can transform your entire self image.

Talk about an esteem booster! This is it right here.

For just a moment, take some time to answer these questions:
- What part did your husband or partner play in forming you in your mother's womb?
- What hand did he have in forming the genetic make up or your personality?
- What board did he sit on to decide your destiny?
- Who asked for his vote when hand picking your mother or your father?

The fact is, neither you nor he had any hand in these matters. This should reinforce the truth that your identity on this earth has always been separate and unique. Surely you should be prized not punched. Treasured not trampled. Celebrated not tolerated.

Obviously the opinions of those we love do count in validating us and so they should, but in a balanced way. All good relationships are built on areas of unity and agreement. I understand that none of us are a law unto ourselves nor an island and I am certainly not advocating anarchy *but* to be honest, if the whole 'regime' stinks,...then let us clean it up.

It's ok that we want to honour our husbands and loved ones. I agree that we should not seek to intentionally offend him or anyone and it is perfectly natural for us to wish to please him. After all, our greatest desire should always be to make our relationships work. This being understood, the point I am trying to make is this: as women, we must be careful not to permit these healthy desires to become a carte blanche license for abusive husbands to use as a weapon of destruction against us.

So please realise, that taking steps to rebuild your self worth in your own eyes is not a useless exercise. Rather it is the inner strength you are going to draw upon in getting help before it is too late.

How do you see yourself?

Now be truthful. When you look at your life, how do you see yourself? How do you measure your worth as a human being?

Do you see yourself as just one of a crowd? No one special? Unimportant? Nothing much to offer?

Have you fallen into the trap of calculating your worth in terms of the amount of the money or possessions you own?

Perhaps you glean your significance from the family you were born into or have now married into?

What is more important to you? Your personal safety and life security or the perceived reputation you may have in society? Which would you rather choose? A title and highly regarded position in the community versus finding a lasting solution to your dilemma?

Sadly, no man made position, material possession, education or even family name will shield you from experiencing an abusive relationship.

Though it happens primarily to women, these days men are also suffering. Domestic violence and abuse affects people from every background, culture and social strata. The rich, the poor and everyone in between. Every religious and faith community is affected. Being a law-abiding citizen, charitable, with all good intentions does not shield you. Not even being a prayerful, Holy Ghost-filled, tongue-speaking Christian makes you exempt.

Basically wherever there are people, domestic violence exists in some form within society. The only solution is to *deal with it* and work towards helping the victim and the perpetrator.

I Have Decided to Accept Myself

Where I come from
And the heritage I bear
My looks, my shape
My weight and my hair
My accent, my tastes
My true nationality
The way I am wired
And my core personality
For there is no copy
I'm one of a kind
A true work of art
God's beloved mastermind

By Vivien Rose

CHAPTER 2

No Excuses!
Abuse is Unacceptable

Have you ever said or thought these words? *"If I can only do things a little better next time, then maybe he will stop hurting me?*

Or … "If only I was … thinner…, better looking… more educated… a great cook… a better lover… earned more money… able to get pregnant… had a baby boy… was more submissive… then maybe the abuse will stop."

Listen!! The list is endless. All the above have been used by one person or the other as a weapon to justify abusing someone else, but none are acceptable.

What excuse has been used against you? Whatever it is, the first step to getting help is that you must face the facts that *there is no acceptable excuse for allowing yourself to be abused in any shape or form.* You must take responsibility for what you permit in your life. It may seem like your choices are limited. But a tough choice *is* a choice. A difficult choice is still a choice.

I am not denying we can all improve in certain areas. Of course we can. However why should your 'improvement' be the condition set before you are treated fairly with kindness and respect? We have already ascertained that you were born with intrinsic value and dignity. You are already one of a kind. This in itself is enough.

Let me ask you a question that was posed to me. "Why do we love babies?"

As I pondered this question, I instinctively thought "No reason, just because". Think about it. What have babies done right or what have they done wrong? Nothing. Yet, there is no denying that for the most part, newborn babies are treasured and loved by those who have them. Simply because they are new human beings brought into the world and human life is precious.

Another story I read beautifully demonstrates this point. A certain man was making a speech and took out a fifty dollar note from his pocket.

He tore the note; trampled on it; smeared it in the dirt; stuck it back together and then held it up for the audience to see. Then he asked a question. "What's the value of this note?" The answer came back. Fifty Dollars Despite being given the rough treatment, its value never changed.

Similarly, our value in life does not deteriorate with age or maltreatment. Life may trample on us and leave us the worse for wear. Yet our inherent value remains intact. We are not defined by what happens to us or by how people choose to validate us.

There is no question you will need to muster a high degree of courage and emotional strength in order to overcome domestic violence or any other form of abuse. Therefore it is vital to consistently remind yourself – 'I am worth it!'

You could start by changing the bad habit of excusing him every time he flies off the handle and start telling yourself – no excuses! Abuse is inacceptable. Always.

CHAPTER 3

Take Cover ... Quickly!

At the *first* opportunity, you need to seek refuge. Take cover means, that until you take steps to distance yourself from the abuser; change rarely comes.

This is especially true if you have been in a relationship for a while. The dynamics of abuse are such that, the first time comes as a shock. Then, after the profuse apologies and the *'I will never do it again'* promises, the abuse continues. Sometimes infrequently. Sometimes in rapid succession. In the majority of cases, the longer you do nothing about it, the worse it gets.

What I did, and what many women do is we believe the promises and the constant apologies without demanding a commitment from our husband or partner to get help. Then later, their sincere apologies eventually turn to blame. You are the reason they do it. You are the problem. It is all your fault. *Now* you are in the danger zone. Because you are subtly being influenced to believe that if only *you* improved, *then* the abuse will stop.

But this is a lie. It's a cover-up for each slap, each punch, each wounding word, and each painful episode.

A very interesting statement was made by Apostle Paul:

> **Ephesians 5:11** *"And have no **fellowship** with the unfruitful works of darkness, but rather expose them."*

The secret to ending an abusive relationship is revealed in this scripture. We must refuse to continue romancing *('fellowshipping')* with the secrecy, fear and intimidation of the perpetrators of domestic violence. Rather we must expose the truth by taking a stand and making it clear to our husband or partner that we will *not* remain silent. Secondly, we must actively seek outside help. When we do nothing, it is tantamount to us becoming an accomplice to an evil work.

If you saw your friend or perhaps a close relative being attacked, would you remain silent? Or would you react by taking steps to stop the attack immediately? If you couldn't physically help, most likely you would call for help to passers by or even call the police.

Why then are we not just as quick to do the same

for ourselves? Why the reticence? This is the paradox of many women in an abusive relationship.

As I have already said in the previous chapters, the onus is squarely on you, the sufferer, to get help. Many times we expect the other person to make the first move but realistically, you must admit that both of you are caught up in a destructive pattern which is difficult to resolve between the two of you alone.

> **Proverbs 22:3** warns us: *"prudent men foresees evil and hides himself, but the simple pass on and are punished."*

This wisdom can definitely be applied to cases of prolonged domestic violence. Once you identify a pattern of abuse in your relationship, you are doing yourself and your partner a disservice by ignoring it or taking no action.

Though you may feel that you are being victimised, what I have discovered is that, in an abusive relationship, there are two malfunctioning individuals involved. You and him.

I am in no way excusing what has happened to you. Neither do I condone violent behaviour.

What I am saying is that if your relationship has got to the stage where outbursts of violent behaviour have become '*normal*' in your home, then both of you are partially to blame.

The perpetrator of violence is to blame for not exercising self control over his or her emotions and for completely disrespecting you as an individual.

However, let us also face up to the uncomfortable fact that we who are victimised are partially at fault as well. Abuse sufferers often contribute to their own demise by simply not taking action after experiencing several bouts of violent behaviour from their partners. It is true that failing to be proactive in this regard usually serves to strengthen abuse, not prevent it.

When we permit violence to continually be used against us without grave repercussions being brought to bear on our relationship; we have unconsciously sent a message to our partner saying:

"Don't worry. It's not that bad. You are allowed to disrespect me in this way. The best way to intimidate me is to bully me and beat me. I may not like what you are doing, but I hate the thought of speaking out even more so I'll keep my mouth shut. Carry on. I won't tell. So you have a license to do it again if you like – with no consequences"

Ouch! Reading it in the first person hurts doesn't it? We would never actually voice those words. That would be ridiculous. But do you realise, that in letting it go – taking no action – covering up bruises – refusing to get help and staying in that situation – this is exactly the message you are conveying.

Getting help doesn't necessarily mean you are getting a divorce. That's what many women fear. It also doesn't necessarily mean taking legal action against your husband or partner. These are things you may have to consider, but not till much later on down the road.

Right now, the motive for getting help should be first and foremost one of safety. You need to get to a place where things can cool down, where you are not under a constant threat of violence and where you are not being tempted to respond in kind.

Believe you me; I gave as good as I got in the early days. There is a dent on the wall from a plate I threw at my husband! Thank goodness there were no children around in those days. If you do have children, the situation is even more urgent.

Domestic violence is the cause of hundreds of injuries and fatalities in the world. It can get rough and God forbid that any one of you takes a life.

As I was writing this book, I read a recent newspaper article which stated that over 300,000 children in the UK have been injured trying to stop arguments and violence between adults at home. Things have gotten so bad that a children's charity NSPCC (National Society for the Prevention of Cruelty to

Children) in the UK is now calling for the issue of domestic violence to be included in the school curriculum with more support given to victims.

I personally know of stories where women have actually suffered other health problems due to constant abuse they suffered without proper help. So never think abusive tendencies won't escalate. How do you know?! What I am discussing could literally be the difference between life and death.

By making the choice to get help, you could save your life, protect your children and even salvage your marriage or relationship. By doing nothing, you risk losing all three.

In many countries, domestic violence is against the law. Therefore, there are usually organisations that can help you in the first instance. Before our separation, I went to a local advisory service for some free impartial advice.

I really did not want my marriage to break up but I had to do something. During our first separation, I decided against Legal action but made a decision to go and live with my sister for a while until I got my thoughts together. I had a three month old baby at that time which spurred me into action with a greater urgency. Children are so often the innocent victims of abusive relationships and I believe you must do everything in your power to protect them from harm.

Part of the fight to rid relationships of the scourge of violence includes helping women to arm themselves with the correct information. Sources of help include free Volunteer Advice Services, Solicitors, Local Councils, Domestic Violence Charities, all easily found on the Internet or Local Libraries.

These organisations can educate you on the options available to you from placing injunctions on your current home, if you intend to remain there, to what are your rights under the law. They can also assist you in locating available refuges in your area if you so require or point you in the direction of any financial assistance you may apply for.

Don't overlook help that is available to you closer to home. Such as, a trusted family member, extended family, friends or leaders in your faith community who would be willing to assist you or at least guide you in the right direction.

The important thing is, you must get help and quickly. I realise many people, even in the church do not like to talk about this issue; subsequently many churches are not properly resourced to handle cases like this. Nonetheless on the positive side, the spiritual and emotional prayer support you receive from loving Christians is definitely a great benefit.

Here is another word of caution. You may have been brought up in a family or be part of a traditional or religious culture where women are looked upon as less important than men. It is very easy in such cultures for women to be silenced by their surrounding environment.

If you are one of these ladies, just accept, it will not feel comfortable for you to buck the system. I found out from personal experience that the mindsets of some people were already geared towards excusing the man and laying the blame on the woman. Traditionally where my husband and I are from, women are expected to tolerate a high degree of male chauvinism.

After all, our mothers bore it, as did our grandmothers; like many women before them; carrying the burden of prejudice and tradition that silenced their right to be valued, respected and heard. So the unspoken question becomes *'why can't we modern ladies also just put up and shut up?'* But this is where the foundation of your actions must be firmly rooted in the knowledge of the truth. The truth becomes your defence.

The truth is, it is not acceptable in the sight of our Creator; who made both male and female; for any one gender to maltreat the other. Have confidence in this.

In fact the bible is clear in pointing out that any leadership conferred upon a man must be used to serve others in love. Jesus Himself said:

> ***Mark 10:42-44*** *"You know those who are considered rulers over the Gentiles, lord it over them, and their great ones exercise authority over them.* ***Yet it shall not be among you****; but whoever desires to become great among you shall be your servant. And whoever of you desires to be first shall be your servant."*

May I also point out that scripture clearly commands wives to *'submit to their husbands as unto the Lord'* and bestows the headship of the home onto the husband. However men are not left to guess or arbitrarily choose for themselves the manner in which they run their relationships. Oh no! Contrary to the traditional and cultural mindsets that exist out there in the world, husbands are specifically *commanded to love* their wives:

> ***Ephesians 5:22-25*** *"Husbands,* ***love your wife****, just as Christ also loved the church and gave Himself for her."*

So then, we may conclude that the expected conduct and set standard for Godly leadership is *Love* and *Service*. Not bullying and beating! There is a deep call among the nations for governments to establish laws upholding gender equality across the board. I believe this is because, there is something in us as people that cries out for justice and equality. Our roles may differ but the question remains, why should that demean us as women? Instinctively we tend to feel dishonoured whenever we are not given equal opportunity, equal validation and equal rights.

So bear in mind, initially you may feel very much alone but keep talking until someone listens. It can be very disheartening when people begin to ask questions like *"what did you do to make him angry"* or *"why can't you just let it go".* People will question your motives and your sincerity. At times, you may be made to feel you are doing the wrong thing and you are being vindictive. It is truly amazing how people react.

I experienced a myriad of reactions from people such as shunning me, isolating me, rejecting any notion anything untoward is going on and using disapproval tactics to try and shame me to be quiet. So I really do empathise with you and know first hand how hurtful and cruel certain comments and reactions can be, especially when you are desperate.

Always keep at the forefront of your mind, the thought that, your actions are helping you put an end to the abuse. You will protect yourself and your children and cause your husband or partner to confront their own behaviour.

I am a great believer in the power of prayer and have seen wonderful results over the years of answered prayers. So continue to pray for your relationship if you are able, but remember *"Faith without works is dead"*

> **James 2:26** *"For as the body without the spirit is dead, so faith without works is dead also."*

Likewise, prayer not backed up by action is impotent. If the first person doesn't help you, go to the second, and the third, until you are satisfied with the solutions being offered. Continued violence is not an option.

Another part of the *works* is establishing respectful rules of conduct and communication with your husband You cannot circumvent his free will but you can help him understand, how his behaviour affects you and hold him accountable. Without accountability, how can there be any admittance or acceptance of error on his part?

You will find that when you discuss your situation with an objective third party, you will get a clearer perspective, which will enable you to make better decisions concerning the way forward.

In many public places these days, there are notices up advising you of where to go or who to call to get help.

In the heat of the moment, when you are under attack and feel trapped – call the Police! Do whatever it takes to get yourself out of harm's way. Surely this is better than suffering loss of limb or life. The good thing about the Police is that you can call them at short notice, any time of day or night and they respond quickly.

They will usually diffuse the situation and take steps to ensure no further violence erupts that day or night. This may mean that one of you agrees to sleep somewhere else for the night which may pose a slight inconvenience. But at least, sanity has been restored and you can take it from there.

Domestic Violence is a potentially explosive situation which could blow up at any time, so please take cover… quickly!

Sources of Help

www.direct.gov.uk
Domestic Violence – protecting yourself and getting help

www.refuge.org.uk
Refuge is a national charity for women and children experiencing domestic violence and abuse. Provides safe accommodation

www.NCDV.org.uk
National Centre for Domestic Violence. Excellent for helping you write a concise statement of what actually took place. They can even help with injunctions and connect you with impartial legal advice.

www.safe4all.org
Support and & help for abused men and women.

www.ignitebenevolencefund.org
IGNITE Benevolence Fund Should you wish to contact me personally with your questions or feedback.

www.facebook.com/pickingupthepieceshelpdesk
"Picking Up the Pieces" Connect with me on FACEBOOK.Daily posts instilling hope, inspiration and motivation in the heart of people going through painful and difficult times.

CHAPTER 4

Recognising an Abusive Mindset

The fight against domestic abuse is far from one-dimensional. It takes personal conviction, courage and action. You will most definitely need third party support and advice and an emotional and physical place of refuge. Finally you may need to employ the assistance of the law enforcement and legal agencies in your fight for security and liberty from domestic abuse.

I don't want to sugar coat it for you. It is an uphill battle. As one kind lady once told me, it's a rocky road ahead. But the prize of freedom from abuse, restoration of your dignity, a life filled with peace and happiness is the victory you are striving for and it is worth it.

What is the alternative? You remain where you are suffering in silence; not only endangering your life but also the lives of your children (for those who are blessed to have them). The marriage or relationship you are clinging onto is being poisoned by the pain and shame of abuse leaving you feeling depressed and desperate or worse still, suicidal.

First we must recognise and understand the *modus operandi* of an abusive mindset. It is always easier to defeat an opponent once you know their game plan. I learned this information first hand from my own life and also from listening to the stories of other women who have come out of similar abusive relationships.

Physical Violence

The most easily identifiable symptom is physical violence. Whether it happens rarely or frequently is not the point. My personal policy has become *zero-tolerance* in this area. In the beginning I wouldn't bat an eyelid at slapping his face if he swore at me or hitting him back. My attitude was nobody could hit me and get away with it. His view was, the rougher he got, the quicker I would calm down and back off. But honestly, I wouldn't recommend either standpoint now.

Adopting a zero-tolerance policy sets up clearly defined boundaries and provided you can stick to it; this will avoid things plummeting out of control. Engaging even in the slightest act of violence can quickly spiral downwards. So if you are able to discuss and agree on this, it will save you much heartache in the future.

In our case, we did have the heart-to-heart talk and agreed during the initial stages of our marriage to 'no more hitting'. Alas I stopped, he didn't.

Verbal abuse

It is not unusual for physical violence to be partnered with verbal and emotional attacks as well. Thankfully I was spared sexual abuse which I have learned is often prevalent.

When he is angry he may say something like *"you are useless"*, *"ugly"*, *"no-good"*, *"and unable to cope on your own"*, *"a failure"*. If you fight or answer back, you are then accused of being *"mad, crazy or imagining things"*. Abusers don't like discussion or debate. They want your total obedience even when what they are asking you to do is wrong. Your viewpoint carries little weight when they are caught up in this mindset.

Typically he may belittle you publicly or resort to tactics such as intentionally shaming or humiliating you before the children. In the end, one of the biggest motivators for me to get out became seeing the dismay and grief my little girls suffered. It became intolerable in my sight. They are innocent and loved both of us, so it was wrong for them to witness what they were being put through.

Often abusive attacks are explosive, ignited by a

small infringement or innocuous remark. They may be accompanied with threats of more harm if you "talk" or mocking words if you put up any type of a resistance. The specifics vary in each case, but you can be sure that every attempt to ridicule you is basically aimed at damaging your self belief and self worth.

Instinctively those who abuse know they must use fear in order to prevent their victims from speaking out or taking action against them.

Men who verbally abuse are alarmingly good with words. They are experts at turning any argument in their favour and can actually give you convincing reasons why their abusive treatment towards you is right and why you are wrong. Words are used as their weapon to wound and debilitate your emotions which makes it harder for you to defend yourself because you are so hurt.

The power of words becomes like a double edged sword in the mouth of the verbal abuser. He can slice your heart with deadly accuracy then in another scenario, he is able to use words to win you over when things are sweet. It's a perfected art I observed first hand.

The verbal abuse had longer reaching effects on me than the physical attacks. Thankfully my bruises healed, and the worst I suffered was concussion, swelling and inability to use my arm for a period of time. I in no way wish to detract from the severity of the attacks themselves. I know that I have been undeniably fortunate in this regard. When I look back now, I can only marvel how I escaped so lightly, given what I was confronted with all those years.

Nevertheless, I have no words to accurately explain the devastation of verbal abuse. If you are experiencing verbal abuse, I feel, there is more of an urgency for you to seek help. It is even more imperative to act now, since this form of attack tends to strip you of all emotional strength and willpower. Once your inner resolve is weakened, you become vulnerable to a state I call – total surrender. A place where you give up your life and liberty to the monster of abuse indefinitely and all hope is lost.

My main defence

If I was asked to disclose, what my biggest defence against verbal abuse was, I would say, the word of God. For it enabled me to continually withstand the barrage of verbal attacks I endured over the years. It was definitely the reason I seemed to remain strong for so long. Moreover, the word of God helped me recover and recuperate even while I was still at risk. It became my invisible shield.

People say to me all the time *"we never knew"* or

"it didn't show" and I can only attribute this to the power of the scriptures applied to my life daily. Right where you are, you can begin to do the same thing.

I didn't just read the bible, I believed it. I spoke it over myself. I rehearsed it daily in my mind. I clung to it with all my heart. The promises in it became my light in a very dark place; my hope for eventual release and the words of Jesus were my source of joy and strength. From this experience, I came to truly understand what Apostle Paul meant when he described the word of God as *'living and powerful'* (Hebrews 4:12). It is just that.

When you pray the scriptures, you are literally praying the mind and will of God into your situation. You are summoning the Highest Authority over all the universe to act on your behalf. Don't just rely on your own natural vocabulary which is limited, pray the word!

Even if you only pray and rehearse one scripture, you are releasing supernatural power which will be enough to keep you until you can get out! I am willing to send you a _free copy_ of the scriptures that helped me. To request your copy, simply email office@igbfund.org and ask for "Scriptures to overcome Abuse".

Meanwhile, here is one effective and powerful

word of assurance from the book of Isaiah:

> **Isaiah 43:2-3** *"When you pass through the waters, I will be with you. And through the rivers, they shall not overflow you. When you walk through the fire, you shall not be burned, Nor shall the flame scorch you, For I AM the Lord your God, the Holy One of Israel, your Saviour." Amen.*

Thankfully I had already become a committed Christian before we married. This decision to follow Christ literally saved my sanity and my health. It is only when you come under constant attack that you can truly appreciate the shield of faith.

The words I read enlightened me, reconstructed my erroneous thought patterns and gave me the power to stand up, get up and fight my way out of the clutches of domestic abuse. I saw what it really meant to be loved. I experienced it firsthand in times of prayer and worship. Whatever evil was perpetrated against me, the Lord always worked something to favour me. He would give me comfort and counter the effects of the abuse on my mind and heart plus on many occasions, He would intervene in miraculous ways. This whole experience has been an eye-opener and a source of wonder to me until today.

He (God) really does see everything and works

with you in whatever state you find yourself. I came to the place where I didn't doubt myself anymore. I trusted He cared for my life over and beyond my marriage which is what so many people seemed more concerned about. I made peace with the fact that I may not be popular for taking a stand but knew I must strive for better. I owed myself and the children that much. This was not Gods best for me, so I chose not to settle for it.

I got tired of tolerating the cycle of abuse. Tolerating the short lived apologies – the fragile peace – the controlling behaviour – the refusal to discuss anything without verbal or physical outbursts – the constant false accusations – the public pretence – the counselling with embellished stories and enforced apologies. Above all the abuse represented total betrayal of our marital vows. It was unacceptable.

Obviously I still had to walk out the process but with every step, the Lord has been there for me and He will be there for you as well. His spirit is love. He is gentle not harsh. He is accepting not condemning and He is merciful not unforgiving. This was the crux of it all. If the *Creator*, our Father in Heaven, treated me with honour, why on earth would I accept anything less from one of his own "created human beings". Nothing, absolutely nothing gave him the right, nor the license to continue in this vein so I chose not to permit it any longer. I voted with action not words.

God is impartial, loving good and hating evil. So once you choose to resist what is wrong, He will extend immeasurable grace towards you which will empower you to do whatever is necessary to get free. But as I said earlier, the decision is down to you. Be warned, your passivity and inertia equals surrender. Any complacency on your part will constrain and limit what people can do to assist you, especially when you refuse to act.

> **James 2:17** *"Thus also, faith by itself, if it does not have works (corresponding action) is dead."*

So you see, you are not waiting for God to do something, He is waiting for you. Stop waiting for something or someone to change. The change you are yearning for begins with what you do.

Behavioural Traits

We've already highlighted some traits of shaming and ridicule. Here are some others to watch out for.

Tearful Apologies

Men who are prone to abusive behaviour also seem to have a habit of apologising in tears hours or days later and promising 'NEVER to do it again'. Two things to watch for regarding his apology. It's normally in private only. Secondly, the blame is pinned on what you *"should have"* done, *"could have"* done or *"did not"* do. This half-baked confession is generally void of any true responsibility. The apology may sound innocent enough until you have the opportunity to sit before a qualified counsellor or third party to discuss your problems.

Suddenly the heartfelt tears and pleadings vanish. In its place you may see total denial, vicious commentary on all your short-comings and false accusations which are levied to discredit your account of events.

Any apology he makes without committing himself to get honest and seek help is basically lip-service. One of the first signs he will show when he is genuinely remorseful will be open, honest confession and admittance of his behaviour. Without blame.

Just as you must take full responsibility for your part in this whole charade. He must own up to his part as well. Fair and square. Remember, as long as he sees *'fit'* to do what he is doing and can justify it to himself or anyone else, the abuse will continue.

Fabrications and False Accusations

Naïvely, I actually thought by seeking the intervention of an objective counsellor, my husband and I would work towards restoring our marriage. It's laughable now but at the time, it never even occurred to me he may lie. Much less did I fathom his inner motives. So initially I went into each counselling session like a 'lamb to the slaughter'.

Please don't skip these steps. Taking a matter before two or three objective witnesses is biblical. This is the best way to decipher the chances of redeeming your relationship so don't opt out. Matt 18:13-19 gives us a step-by-step grievance procedure, detailing how believers are to deal with conflict and disputes. It is imperative to note that, once a believer refuses to comply with godly counsel, we are given two final instructions to: (a) treat them like unbelievers and (b) draw a line in the sand against behaviour that is not permissible.

To my chagrin, scenes and stories were fabricated and words were taken out of context. The report of entire events was turned upside down and inside out. After sitting through conflict resolution sessions with senior members of our family, concerned friends and spiritual leaders over several years, I eventually came to the place where it seemed futile. After years of refusing to press charges against him – despite police pressure to do so – my own husband pressed assault charges on me! This was probably my lowest moment. I was in absolute disbelief. It was then that it hit me: *whatever it took* for him to cover his tracks, he would do it.

Recognise this response from the aggressor is not unusual. Shocking but not uncommon. You are endangering your life, hoping against hope for a miraculous change. Meanwhile he may still be living in denial, unwilling to admit or confront the obvious, talk less of changing.

Dual Personality

This one is a biggie. I observed this characteristic in action over fourteen years so became well acquainted with it. One major symptom of abuse is that your husband or partner will go to extraordinary lengths to ensure their cover is not blown. The key to recognising his dual personality does not lie in what he tells you in private but in how he responds in public when he is confronted or the abuse is revealed.

Is he remorseful and repentant? Does he accept any responsibility for his abusive behaviour or is he in complete denial? Does he become vindictive and malicious? Don't be too disheartened if he reacts this way. At first, it came as a massive blow to me as well. The reality is, this tendency is a major trait, learned and adopted by all types of abusive people per se. Just think about it. People given to abuse must learn how to "disguise" that part of their personality otherwise they would not be able to continue undetected for years!

Rarely do they reveal the abusive side of their nature in public. When they do, it is usually due to a momentary relapse when they were taken off guard. Even in those moments, they tend not to concede any guilt but will emphatically deny or excuse away their behaviour with a plausible reason. Another way they react is to take steps to avoid the company of those who suspect something is going on.

This is why the onus is not just on the abuser to change. The onus is also on the person who is suffering. Collectively the onus is on your circle of family and friends, on the community, on the government and on society at large. We all have a part to play. My thoughts are, because the effects of domestic violence are so wide reaching and damaging, we all have a shared responsibility to do our utmost to help bring it to an end once we sense something or know something, we should do something. Failing to act is surrender. We simply should not ignore it!

I am persuaded that one of the major reasons why many women suffering from domestic violence, do not come forward sooner, is because they are concerned nobody will believe them. Faced with a choice between the charming, loveable public persona of the man they know versus the possibility this man is abusive in private, people don't want to believe you!

It is difficult to comprehend at the best of times. So admittedly, the prospect of not being believed can be a daunting one since it presents us with the added challenge of fighting to be heard.

Nevertheless we must persist in exposing the truth and I encourage you to push through anyway. It is so easy to waste precious time, getting caught up with anxiety as we keep stressing over who does or doesn't believe us. At some point you must realise that endless discussions and opinions over the *whats*, *whys* and *wherefores* are simply diverting your focus from the main issue. My recommendation is you spend your energy on the more productive process of acting on what you *know* to be true regardless of what onlookers are thinking or saying.

In short, by keeping silent, you are essentially providing a cosy environment for the deceitful nature of abuse to grow. Moreover you are placing yourself and your kids in jeopardy. Counselling may help and prayer is laudable. These are both necessary as a means to inject wisdom, divine insight and grace into your situation.

However, until you take a more proactive approach to confront and deal with domestic abuse, it does not end. In fact, your silence can be read as the *green light'* for him to continue maltreating you. It's that simple. So I urge you once again – for both your sakes – take that first step to get help. You will safeguard your life, the lives of your children *and* you may just save your marriage as your exit may challenge him to consider his ways.

CHAPTER 5

The Natural, Hurtful and Helpful Response

The Natural Response

When we become desperate for our relationship to work, there is a natural tendency for us to try increasingly harder to stop *pushing his buttons*. Before long we build up a list of topics or issues to be avoided and we resort to lengthy tactics to *keep the peace*.

What I have discovered is that the dynamics of abuse changes as things worsen. The natural response is limited in the long run because whatever made him angry today may not necessarily be the trigger point for him tomorrow. Therefore you are left in a constant state of anxiety over how he will react in any given situation and your freedom of expression is eroded day by day.

The Hurtful Response

The hurtful response is when we always seek to appease him or acquiesce to every demand, especially if pleasing him demeans your self respect.

Oddly enough, giving in to his every whim and demand doesn't guarantee the abuse will stop. I found that if I agreed to his demands, all would be sweet for a season. But soon, he would demand more… and more… yet these demands rarely took my interests or viewpoint to heart.

Along with physical and verbal abuse comes passive control. It's hard to comprehend exactly why our husbands resort to domestic abuse and even harder for people to really appreciate from the outside why women stay. But at the root of it all is the issue of *control*. If you have been in an abusive relationship for any length time, you do see a pattern emerging.

Abusive men are very controlling. Anytime your spouse wants to subvert your will or manipulate your mind, this in essence, is the spirit of control. We are all born into this world with a free will, proven by the fact that, even babes in arms can throw tantrums! Funny to watch but they do.

Our will is meant to be exercised freely not under coercion or manipulation. So when someone expects you to surrender your choices to them against your will, recognise this as the spirit of control in operation. The more you resist, the more reason the aggressor is given to use physical force, violence or other methods of abuse to gain the upper hand. Control can manifest overtly or covertly. It is not always with aggression but could manifest as passive aggressive. This happens when a person freezes you out emotionally or simmers quietly as a warning sign telling you that, they are not pleased! If you ignore the warning signals, you are punished by their withdrawal of affection, attention, finance or whatever hurts you most.

Common areas your husband or partner may seek control are over matters of finance; what you spend – down to the last penny. Should you dare go over the budget even a fraction; world war three may ensue. This is an imbalance.

He may want to control where you go, who you see and what you wear. In the bedroom he may dictate when and how often you sleep with him. All married couples have points of difference or debate. But you can recognise there is a problem when decisions almost always *contravene your will*. If you feel bullied, scared, manipulated or threatened into submission, there is an issue of control.

An area I found difficult to navigate was when I felt my husband wanted to control what I liked, what I believed, and what I thought. If our opinions differed he sometimes saw that as an infringement on his authority and violence often followed. If I stated my preference for a place, person or programme, it could cause enough friction for an outburst. My initial reaction was to appease him. But as I read, prayed and grew in wisdom, it became evident to me that my response was actually hurtful in that it fed his lust for control.

Without the safety net of healthy boundaries, human desires tend to grow into an insatiable monster which eventually leads to abuse. This is true of all our appetites. Hence thousands in our society suffer from one form of addiction or another. All are expressions of abuse. Self inflicted or not. The best way we can circumvent these tendencies is to exercise self control. Dealing with domestic abuse is no different.

Rather than appease, we must attempt to reinstall and reinforce healthy boundaries such as respect and consideration back into our relationship. Obviously there exists an imbalance due to the fear and intimidation of violence and abuse. I understand this too well. Only you can make the judgement call whether to resist or desist. Quite frankly there are times, it is best to just get out of the way.

Yet whenever possible, it is still worth your while insisting on respect by firmly expressing your viewpoint. By standing your ground, you are reaffirming your stance as a person worthy of consideration. After all, marriage does not give him an open license to rail road you into accepting every decision, whim and desire. It should be a loving, growing partnership between two individuals facing the world together, not fighting against each other.

The Helpful Response

As a person I am naturally very forthright and persistent and I am always willing to try. My attitude tends to be, If it will work or make things better, why not? But after fourteen years of umpteen infractions, counselling, pleading, arguing, police visits, lies, betrayal and false accusations the penny finally dropped – girlfriend, you are fighting a lethal battle! By this time, our relationship was so toxic it was endangering my life and our children lived in fear of the next incident.

The helpful response is when you are able to look for ways to secure your safety without having to go through a fracas, vicious spat or potentially dangerous confrontation.

I did not get clear quickly enough and everything blew up in my face. So my sincere hope for you as you read this book is that you will avoid a similar occurrence.

The day I reacted to counter his attack and picked up a ruler to hit him continuously became the day of enforced decision. I decided; never again will he lay one finger on me. Never again will my children see their beloved daddy hurting their dear mother. Never again will I permit physical violence and verbal abuse to remain in my home. Never again will I put myself at risk of sustaining more injuries or worse still loss of life. And never ever again would I allow pressure to build to the point I would be provoked to do something worse than picking up a ruler!

It simply wasn't worth it. Though I had been threatened with lethal objects in the past, God forbid I or he should cause irreparable harm. Many women are pushed to this point. Statistically *two women* are killed by a current or former partner every week in England and Wales and thirty women a day attempt suicide to escape domestic violence. How much can someone take?! I hope you don't wait to get to that point. Act now to remove yourself from danger. For your sake and for his.

I experimented with every imaginable response known to man and came to the conclusion slowly and painfully that no matter how much you care for someone, unless they are willing to confront their behaviour and take responsibility for their actions, no lasting change can ever occur.

When you love someone and have built a life

together, you have fond memories with them so it is hard to let go. It is not just the death of a marriage, it's the death of a dream. For those of who are grieving through this process, there is hope to salvage your relationship once you have exercised what I call "tough love". After our first lengthy separation, we reunited and tried again. Unfortunately the abuse resurfaced and it is during that period, I learnt the value of tough love.

Exercising Tough Love

Remember your husband or partner, through their habitual choices have been taken captive by the spirit of abuse and also need help. People don't just wake up and begin to maltreat someone they profess to love. It is a gradual process of them needing control and exerting their power over you forcibly which leads them down the path of secrecy, threats and violence.

In some cases, there are external factors such as upbringing, alcoholism, drug addiction, spiralling debt or family pressures which may influence his behaviour towards you.

Notwithstanding, domestic violence and abuse is wrong and keeping silent is not the answer. Hence the need for tough love.

Tough Love doesn't hang on to what is detrimental

at all costs. Tough love rejects destructive behaviour. Tough love cares enough to say "No". Tough love demands a degree of discipline. If boundaries are continually broken, tough love is strong enough to let the person face the consequences. Tough love is not malicious nor wicked. It doesn't delight in causing pain or suffering, nor does it harbour grudges when the person sincerely repents. Rather tough love seeks to protect what is left in the hope that its recipient will be brought back from the verge of destruction. Tough love understands that setting boundaries is essential to maintaining a safe and peaceful environment.

Parents teach this concept to their children and governments set laws using this principle. In fact there is no institution or relationship on earth which runs well without adopting a system of accountability.

Under normal circumstances, people who misbehave are made well aware they can expect to be disciplined or receive a warning. At home, we only have to ask the children who have been grounded. In our workplaces, there are people who have been dismissed for a misdemeanour. Another example practised by our society is that, those that are charged with criminal activity are sent behind bars. Everyone is accountable to someone, legally, socially and morally.

In reality, we accept that the absence of a penalty

effectively means, there is often not enough incentive for people to do right or to change. Likewise an abusive partner needs to understand, there is a limit they should not go beyond. If they disregard healthy boundaries, there must be a penalty. For serial offenders, the most loving thing you can do is remove them or yourself from the equation.

The Abuser's Response

Once you make your response, you can expect one of two reactions. He may rant and rave initially but once the dust has cleared, he may weigh up the possibility of losing you altogether and decide to seek help. This is fantastic and should be encouraged and celebrated because this means, in some way, he still values and cares for you enough to fight for your relationship.

Alternatively, his abusive behaviour will escalate into Acts of Betrayal.

Acts of Betrayal

I encountered the heat of this immediately after we separated the second time and a non-occupancy injunction was placed on my husband. Every venomous attack in the book was used. My name was defamed to anyone and everyone who would listen and concur. False reports were circulated among our community, church members and friends. Court cases ensued with realms of written statements detailing things I had allegedly done. To top it all, we lost our business, our cars and eventually our home since he refused to make payment towards anything.

I have since discovered that many abusers embark on hate campaigns to discredit their wife's name among friends, family and their social circle. I had people knocking on my door; people with whom I had never ever discussed or exposed my marital affairs to; telling me off because my husband had talked to them for hours about how I was maltreating him! No mention is made of all the provocations you were given over the months and years by the way. Believe me it can get ugly.

As I said before, it was a rocky road but one well worth travelling. By relaying these events, I want you to be prepared for the worst even as you hope for the best. Whatever he chooses to do, you do what is right for yourself and your family.

Without going into detail about every situation, I just want you to realise, it may start as a slap, a punch, or him swearing at you whenever he is angry. But if left unchecked, abusive tendencies don't just go away.

In time, our joint dreams and aspirations began to wither and before long, our marriage became the breeding ground for mistrust and resentment which are ugly by-products of domestic abuse.

The death knell for our marriage came after fourteen years of fighting the plague of domestic abuse. Like a cancerous growth, violence and abuse in a relationship has the potential to mar and destroy every good thing of what was once a loving, fun and beautiful relationship. There really is no room for complacency.

Use My Story as your learning curve. Whatever your particular scenario is, you too must accept the fact that you really have no control over what your husband thinks or what he does. You cannot change him and you cannot force him to confront his hurtful behaviour against his will.

As far as it depends on you, live at peace with all men is the biblical advice. There are times though when this is no longer possible. My simple advice remains, once you find yourself in an explosive and abusive situation, it is paramount that you channel your focus and energy on helping yourself and your children secure a safe haven where you have a chance to recover and heal.

If in the process, your husband or partner genuinely decides to deal with his abusive behaviour before seeking a reunion, that's all well and good. Nevertheless, your prime concern right now must be to get to safety.

CHAPTER 6

My Story

In a nutshell this is what happened. We had five years of a rocky marriage, followed by what turned out to be a five-year separation (another book altogether) due to domestic abuse and associated issues. We never divorced but I moved out and told him, until he was willing to seek help, we could no longer live together. It took four years before he came back and apologised. The no-blame apology I was talking about earlier. He accepted help and sought counsel. He had also recommitted himself to the Christian faith a little before that and had received a good report from those who were mentoring him. So much to everyone's surprise and joy, we decided to give our marriage another go.

Though we were not technically divorced, we retook our vows and reunited our family during the tenth year of our marriage. This time round, I was frank about my concerns from the get go and actively sought support. We agreed to establish lines of accountability to our church pastors and family elders right from the onset and to be fair; it helped for a while.

Things were great until the abuse began again after our second child. The support system kicked in and we tried to put the incidents behind us. I had grown wiser now so dealt with things without delay. No more silences. I called for help from those I felt were qualified. However, over the next four years, the bouts of abuse gradually became worse as his respect for the words of the elders and pastors diminished. It can't be said that we didn't receive well meaning or sound advice. We did. But! No amount of discussion could change his heart. His main angst seemed to be, nobody should tell him how to run his home. It was his house, his family and he wanted *no* interference. Fair enough but where did that leave us when he ran out of control, which he did. Who was he accountable to?

Long story short, he surrendered his will to the grip of abusive impulses, control, violence and manipulation. I can not pinpoint the turning point or tell you the exact time his heart changed. He became grieved with so many things, life pressures ensued and like a speeding train, the domestic abuse escalated.

This was the moment I should have exercised tough love. In hindsight, I can see now, without a change of heart, it was foolhardy for me to expect a permanent change of mind.

Let me also appeal to people who are in a position to help. Please if you ever have the opportunity to help someone going through domestic abuse, the worst thing you can do is ostracise them. This applies to males and females.

The men need help along with the women. I am convinced, my husband did not like who he had become. Deep down in his conscious, he was as trapped as I was. As a person, he is extremely capable, intelligent and caring. But this monster of abuse which had started off so small had now taken over his persona and character.

You can help men to recognise the need for help by refusing to condone his behaviour. Men seem reluctant to get involved. There is a natural code of honour between men which infers, I leave you to yours and you leave me to mine. But I believe that men are the answer to helping themselves. Very few men acted to help us. Yet I instinctively feel that a man's voice and authority goes a long way to penetrating the mask of denial which abusers cover themselves. Confession is a huge part of the battle. Encouraging your friend, colleague or brother to admit what he has fallen into could be the catalyst to turning him around and opening him up to consider the option of seeking qualified help.

I found that many people simply do not know how to support those in abusive situations – especially if the man in question is in leadership. It is not uncommon for women to be shunned for daring to speak out.

The standard response became "don't make him angry" or just "pray for him". Other people were more concerned for our "marriage" forgetting our home had become a war zone with real danger and violence. Among the Black Christian community, we are actively encouraged *not* to call the police, yet when you are being threatened with a knife, a pair of scissors, boiling water or your arm is being twisted, these same people do not come to your rescue!

Please be wise. Domestic Violence is one of the leading causes of homicide and murder in the UK and other nations around the world and statistics are on the rise. People may be quick to see your failings, criticise your stance, berate your lack of faith or spirituality but they do not know what you know. They do not see the bleeding hearts, your wounded body or the devastated lives of your children. Worse still are those who see but do not help. Like the parable of the Good Samaritan, they pass by on the other side.

It is your life, so you must make those tough decisions. The final year of our marriage was what I can only describe as "a living nightmare" filled with one traumatic experience after another. In all my days, I have never contemplated suicide but during that period I did feel like I was dying. The acts of betrayal were the worst to bear. But I have made it through and I am truly thankful for my dear friends and select family members who stood by me during that season.

Whether you call it faith or stubbornness, I held on to the end. But the day of final release came one new year when I had confirmation in my spirit I must "let him go" for all our sakes and leave the rest to God.

CHAPTER 7

Walking Out – The Practicalities

Once you have made the decision to get help, you will be faced with sorting out the practicalities of your new life.

Let me reiterate, taking the step of getting to safety will in most cases cause temporary separation but help is available to heal and mend your marriage in time. Many times divorce is not the only solution. We will deal in later chapters with the road to recovery and healing aspect of this journey. For now let's focus on living life without your spouse or partner.

All the considerations we cover in this chapter may not apply to your own personal situation. Some of you may now be single ladies. Whereas others have become single parents. A number of you may still be living in the same house. Others have moved to a new location. In every case, simply take what is of relevance to you.

One of the first priorities that faced me, after finding

shelter at my sister's house, was the challenge of picking up sufficient clothes and toiletries. Then came the issue of finding work, making an income, budgeting, childcare and basically learning how to build a life as a single parent.

Collecting Your Things

I was fortunate enough to be able to arrange to go back to my former house and pick up some essentials. It is always advisable to arrange to pick up your essentials with an escort. Don't go alone. Get the children taken care of, to save them going through any further trauma and pick up *essentials only.*

At the bare minimum you will need:

Toiletries

- Toothbrush/Toothpaste
- Soap
- Sponge or Flannel
- Deodorant
- Shampoo & Conditioner
- 1 Brush & Comb
- 1 set hair bands
- 1 Nail clippers (share)
- Hair cream (if applicable)
- Body lotion

Clothes
- 2 sets nightwear
- 3 sets of underwear
- 1 skirt
- 1 trouser
- 2 shirts/blouses
- 2 jumpers/cardigans
- 1 suit (if you have one)
- School uniform (everything)
- 1 pair low shoes
- 1 pair high heeled shoes
- 1 pair boots
- 1 pair trainers
- 1 warm overcoat

Bed linen
- 1 blanket/duvet
- 1 sheet
- 1 pillowcase

<u>In addition for babies, pack</u>:
- Baby grows
- Nappies
- Wipes
- Formula feed
- Bottles

- Steriliser
- Baby food (bottled)
- Washing up liquid
- Baby cream
- Baby soap, shampoo
- Warm cardigan/jumpers
- Warm coat/snowsuit
- Cot blanket
- Cot sheet
- Cot pillow case

Documents
- Passports
- Driving License
- Lastest bill(s) for ID purposes
- Child Benefit/Tax credits letters
- Proof of benefit letters
- Bank Account details
- 3 months bank statements
- (if possible)
- Credit and Debit Cards

Miscellaneous
- Take your favourite photographs.
- Favourite toy for the children

When I left, I had literally forty-five minutes to

pack what I could for myself and my baby daughter and I did it under Police escort to avoid any ugly confrontations or problems.

The best scenario is to wait until you are sure the house is empty. Either way, ensure you go with an escort if at all possible.

You don't need a lot. Only what is really necessary for survival. This can be quite traumatic, since you will be familiar with life in your home and many of your personal belongings will have to be left behind.

For your own sake, don't overload yourself. Remember wherever you are staying, there usually isn't the space for too many things and if you have to move again, you don't need the added hassle of too much luggage.

Make a clean break. You could probably pack a comforter or favourite toy for the children if they have one, but not every toy and doll! It sounds callous but this is very often the only way to get out swiftly. Your life is your prize. Things can always be acquired again. Think of all those people who have suffered through an earthquake or a flood and lost every material thing including their homes. Yet, they lived on.

So remember, your situation is no less serious. Drastic action is required in order for you to have a fighting chance of making progress in life and building a future for yourself and your children. You will survive. You will recover and you will be ok. I did it. Many others have done it and you can do it too.

Staying Home

If you prefer to stay home, for whatever reason, you will have to get a legal document prohibiting your abusive spouse or partner from inflicting any more physical and verbal abuse on you plus in some cases he may not be allowed to continue living in the house with you. Every case is considered on the virtues of its own merit and the orders will be granted or withheld based on evidence provided and the severity of the abuse suffered.

The type of orders, the courts may consider enforcing are:

- "non-molestation order"
- "non-occupancy order"

Under UK law, these orders do not require you to press criminal charges and they will not give him a criminal record. However, once they are granted and the abusive partner insists on violating the conditions therein, the courts may see fit to charge him with a criminal offence. It is advisable to seek legal assistance and counsel before taking any decision.

The Question of Money

If you are single without children, the challenge of finding work, or creating an income is usually easier.

If you are already working in a steady job, it would be a good idea to maintain your position. However, there are instances where you have to move to a completely new area. This was my situation.

I was not working since I had only recently had a baby three months prior. I was fortunate to qualify for state benefits which was then called income support. This was a minimal amount of approximately one hundred dollars per week which literally paid for my weekly baby expenses and fed us on a shoe-string budget.

Later on, when the baby was a little over a year, I was able to go back to study part time and retrain as a beauty therapist.

The reason I chose this profession was two fold. If I were to maintain my career in hotel management, the hours would have been too unsociable for me to be able to take care of the baby alongside working.

Secondly, I have always had a talent for beauty therapy but never fully released my potential in that field. However, after I qualified, I was able to work part time and build a mobile beauty therapy business with flexible hours. That way I could earn an income and take care of my baby.

Two important lessons I learned were:

- be willing to retrain if necessary in order to make a viable work or business choice.
- work in the area of your gifting, you will naturally improve your chances of success without too much added stress.

Childcare

If you do have children, you must source out inexpensive childcare options in order to release yourself to be available for work. Childcare must be budgeted for.

Before this, be careful to write and let the school or childcare provider know exactly who is and isn't allowed to pick up your children if they are still young. Especially if any legal injunctions have been put in place against your husband or partner. The last thing you want is for your children to be kidnapped or taken without your consent. It happens ladies. All the time. So its good to put measures in place which will work to safeguard your children.

I do not advocate that children should be used as pawns in any relationship breakdown. Rather I believe that, as much as possible, both parties should work to mutually agree times and places for fathers to visit their children and vice versa.

However, the volatile emotions involved in a fresh break up often causes people to act irrationally and if care is not taken, the children may become endangered. My feelings on this are for you to go with your gut instinct. If you sense in any way visitation may become hazardous to the safety of your children, don't ignore your sixth sense. Start off with meeting in public places or under supervision if necessary until you are sure, no harm will come to the children.

I wrote this book in 2009 and 3 years later on the news, we hear weekly reports of incidents involving estranged and enraged parents harming children. Please be careful. Use your common sense.

What are your options? Do you have any family or relatives who can help you with your children? If not, is there a day-care crèche or family centre in your area? By building relationships with other mothers, there may be the option of shared child care of other women's children at certain times in return for them looking after yours when needed.

Alternatively, you may consider qualifying to become a professional child minder. This way, you would be home to take care of your children and still earn an income.

Obviously if you are in a refuge, some of these

options are not available to you. However, the one thing, I strongly advise is, find a practical course teaching a skill that you can offer in the marketplace. Otherwise, you will be perpetually stuck on having a minimal income with few opportunities to expand.

We are fortunate in the UK to have various grants and tax credits geared towards helping with the costs of childcare and lone parent education and training. Take advantage of everything on offer! Be proactive. Go down to your local council and ask them what is available to you. Out of frustration, I went and asked my local job centre how I could start my own business and found specific training courses were available and even business start up grants! I received help with the childcare whilst I attended college two days a week and financial assistance towards the cost of transport which is expensive in London!

Finally be patient. This doesn't happen in a day, or even a month. It took me one year to come to grips with my separation, before I had the strength to look forward and not backward.

Take it one day at a time. Remember you are not just dealing with the practicalities but also working through emotional issues as well.

Budgeting

It is still the case that in many homes, the man is the primary bread winner which means, when a marital relationship breaks down, it is usually the woman who falls into financial hardship.

This is one of the prices we pay for taking a stand. First time we separated, I left with little or no money and it was months before my ex-husband saw fit to provide financially for our daughter.

After reuniting and making a fresh go of things for another four years, our marriage sadly ended. On this occasion, many dirty games were played financially and materially and basically we lost everything we had invested and built up. Nonetheless I knew this was the price I had to pay for my liberty. What was the point of dying prematurely and saving a house or a car. Where there is life, there is hope. You can rebuild, you can buy back material things. You can never replace life. Today I'm still enjoying the blessing of restoration, with the added bonus of living in peace and tranquillity.

Even if your income is drastically reduced, there are some simple steps you can take to improve your quality of life. One of them is budgeting.

You cannot afford to buy without forethought, so

plan your essentials weekly.

Before we separated, I was used to being paid *monthly* and receiving a *monthly* wage and doing my *monthly* shopping.

However, when you are on a small income, you will need to plan everything weekly. Simply because, special offers and prices differ week to week and you can keep a closer eye on what is going on.

I learnt to buy economy food brands. I learnt to shop for essentials when the shops had special offers on. Plus I also became an expert at cooking tinned tuna in many different and creative ways! Tuna with veg. Tuna with pasta. Tuna salad, Tuna mayonnaise sandwiches. Tuna in baked potatoes. Tuna with baked beans. All this from a girl who grew up in a privileged home, had a private education and was used to a sizeable disposable income. If I can do it, so can you. Anyway, at least meals were nutritious but more importantly they were cheap!

Another food that can stretch a long way is rice. One thing I didn't scrimp on was milk, fruit and vegetables, especially when my little one began weaning. There is always one thing or the other on special offer – always!

Fresh Meat and Fish can be a little expensive when you have a small budget but I found an excellent way to cut costs was to buy from the market in bulk and share costs with my family and friends. It usually works out much cheaper than buying individually and you get more for your money as well.

This approach works well for other items as well. Team up with other single mothers in your situation. Don't go it alone. Sometimes you may feel tempted to isolate yourself, but this really is detrimental when you have suffered abuse. Interacting with other people socially and forming friendships and bonds is important to a woman. We are relational beings and need each other. I still thank God for the social network I built up with my friends, sisters and neighbours during that time.

With one lady in particular, I formed a bond for life and today I remain grateful for the support and kindness we shared during our time of need. So extend a hand of friendship to someone else. They will usually respond in kind.

Take Care of You

In the film *Pretty Woman* starring Julia Roberts, the prostitute Vivien and her friend used to have a saying when they were leaving each other – *"take care of you"*. I loved it. My advise exactly. Initially I did not do this part very well at all. Ladies, we know how easy it is to be so busy looking after everyone else, we end up constantly putting our *me-time* on hold.

When you are a single parent, the time and money pressures are multiplied and this can make it even more difficult to look after yourself. So in the midst of all your attempts to sort things out, spend a little time to *take care of you*. It needn't be something extravagant. I used to love to go and get a manicure or pedicure at a place that offered the treatment for just a fraction of a price. Bargain!

Whatever it is you like to do to relax or pamper yourself, take the time to invest back into yourself. Things like reading a book, doing your hair, exercising, relaxing in a bubble bath, watching your favourite film on DVD, socialising with friends, walking in the park or anything that makes you feel good about yourself. Your esteem and self worth have taken a battering and these little steps of pampering and self focus can help to rebuild it again.

Looking back, I realise this step is crucial since it marks the beginning of a much deeper healing process.

CHAPTER 8

The Road to Recovery

The best way I can describe the process of recovering from the emotional, physical and psychological trauma of domestic violence is to compare it to what a person's body goes through after a major operation, accident or health crisis.

By using the word – trauma – I am alluding to the fact that their body is put under a stressful state which interrupts it's normal functioning equilibrium for a season. Their body temperature, blood pressure and skin colour often changes. Their strength is sapped and it is not possible for them to physically exert themselves as they would under normal circumstances. Should the incident be life threatening, drastic measures are taken and they are rushed to the nearest hospital where medical staff do all within their power to stabilise them.

If we are to take this analogy further, we know that after people undergo major surgery, they are given a period of recuperation in the 'recovery room' before being taken to a ward for continued 'bed rest' which could last from a few days to weeks.

Patients are rarely wheeled straight back onto the ward. Reason being, the doctors and nurses wish to check their vital signs are responding well to ensure the operation was successful.

If they notice that the patient is displaying any abnormal vital signs, then this becomes an indication of a greater problem within and the medical staff are alerted to act immediately!

Vital signs are therefore crucial in depicting if a patient is recovering well and will heal in the course of time.

Recovering from a physical sickness has several stages which can be compared to the process of emotional healing and recovery.

Similarly, when you have suffered through an abusive relationship, your emotions are traumatised and they need to gain equilibrium before true healing can begin.

After patients are discharged from hospital, the doctors may advise a further period of rest and recovery at home. They are sensitive to the fact that surrounding conditions either aid or hinder healing, so are always careful to advise patients accordingly. Most importantly they acknowledge healing takes time. Yet fast forward several months or years after major surgery, there is so often, no outward sign of trauma. Perhaps all that remains is a scar and the memory.

The process of recovering from the emotional trauma and psychological distress of an abusive relationship is much the same. Gradually over time, the day will come when you are no longer held bound to old habits and thought patterns that were so prevalent in your past relationship. Your wounds will have healed and you can move on to live a full and productive life.

The steps of recovery for emotional health mirror those required for physical health. You need to give yourself time to work things through. If you have survived through years of abuse, most likely you will have developed some sort of coping mechanism with which to handle the pain. Things like over indulging in food, serial dating, impulsive shopping, alcohol or drug abuse, pity parties, self harm, acting tough, being angry or abusive towards others, shutting yourself off from the outside world, depression, lack of interest in your appearance, fantasizing about the day your partner will suffer harm and the list goes on.

Everyone is different and none of us react in exactly the same way. But there are always tell-tale signs that all is not well. Quite naturally so. After all, you would be superhuman to experience what you have without it negatively affecting your psyche in some way, no matter how strong you are.

Though these mechanisms help us to mask the pain, we know they do not solve the root problem. I truly believe that those women who take the time to heal emotionally and learn from their experiences are the only ones who will benefit in the long run.

A psychiatrist and humanitarian, called Dr Elisabeth Kübler-Ross, pioneered research into the support and counselling of personal trauma and grief, associated with death and dying. Her ideas, notably the *five stages of grief model*, highlighted _denial_, _anger_, _bargaining_, _depression_ and _acceptance_ as common reactions to trauma and grief.

Interestingly, the model identified similar observed reactions by people who were either grieving or confronted with relationship breakdown, redundancy, financial despair and bankruptcy. For this purpose I want us to take a minute to focus on the five cited reactions in regards to relationship breakdown.

Dr Kübler-Ross recognised the stages were not necessarily progressive but rather interchangeable. She states in her findings that not everyone goes though every stages. However the model became a useful tool for helping people work through their grief and personal trauma.

I can certainly relate with these stages as I reflect back on my own road to recovery.

Denial

For me *denial* was definitely the first stage! Somehow we can't believe domestic violence is happening to us and we remain in a state of incredulity and shock. We ask ourselves questions such as *'how could our relationship which started off with so much promise become a living nightmare?'*

Denial was partly the reason I waited five years to take a stand the first time round. I kept hoping against hope that things would just change. Somehow I thought that things would gradually improve until the violence stopped and we would move on. Naïve as it sounds, that's the hope many women cling to.

Coupled with this was my fervent hope that my marriage would not break up. Again I'm sure many women are nodding in agreement as they read this. Worse still, when we add other factors such as fear, a battered esteem and cultural taboos to this deadly mix of emotions, the whole situation becomes a potent recipe for denial and delayed action.

Hopefully the earlier chapters of this book where I

discussed the issues of value, esteem and the importance of taking cover quickly will help you to effectively deal with denial As your comrade in battle, I urge you not to let another day go by without doing something about your situation.

Anger

Now let's talk about *anger*. This emotion is one of my Achilles heel. Some people internalise anger against themselves. Others direct it at others. I was upset with myself for letting things deteriorate to the level they had, and I was *furious* with my husband. Absolutely furious!

I used to lash out in anger at him, insulting him and his family. After all, how could he do this to me? How dare he?! My anger was on more than one level. Firstly, I was angry that my vision of what marriage should be had been smashed to smithereens. Secondly I was angry at the fact that we actually separated at the worst possible time in my view, just three months after having our first child. The second time around, it was when my oldest was nine years old and the baby girl only three. A time when I was not in full time employment and our separation came during a season I had hoped would be a new beginning for us as a family. So many dreams dashed. So much effort, prayer and years of hope simply flushed down the drain. Or so I thought. Looking back, now, I can see that many good things did come from my ordeal but this is in hindsight.

Have you reacted in similar ways? Understandably aggrieved as you feel, be warned – sustained aggressive anger can lead to rage if not dealt with.

Perhaps your tendency is to direct anger inward towards yourself. Women who do this ask questions like *'How could I let this happen?'* – *'What's wrong with me?'* or *'Am I not good enough?'*

This is equally as common a reaction as outward aggression, especially in relationships where the woman feels that she must take sole responsibility for the success of her marriage.

Granted, women wield great influence over the environment and atmosphere of their homes for better or for worse. However, there is also truth in the analogy cited by Dr Myles Munroe, ** who compared marriage to making an omelette. He stated, *"you need two good eggs to make it work. If only one egg is bad, the whole omelette becomes bad"*

Isn't that so true?! It is important for us to realise that husbands and wives have a shared responsibility for building a lasting marriage. No matter how adept you are as a person, you can never be or replace your husband. You can never be a father. Only he can. You can only play the role of wife and mother. So many woman attempt to over compensate for their husband's bad behaviour in a bid to smooth things over in the home. That leads to frustration and exhaustion. Take responsibility for what you do but stop blaming yourself for everything.

Whichever way you tend to manifest your anger; be it inward, outward or a mixture of both; neither are healthy in the long run.

The best way I know to release yourself from anger is forgiveness. Forgiveness may not be easy but it is necessary. More for your own sanity and emotional liberty than anything else. If you hold onto the rancour and bitterness, you are, in essence, surrendering to the fruits of domestic abuse.

I struggled with forgiveness myself which is why I have devoted an entire two chapters of this book discussing the prickly subject. Chapters 10 and 11.

Bargaining

This section brings a smile to my face as I still remember my woeful bargaining! Dr Kübler-Ross observed that many people use the tactic of bargaining in a desperate bid not to lose their relationships. Some bargain for friendship, others promise to *do anything* and if we are honest we also resort to bargaining with

God. All this in an effort to bring relief. A fast, quick escape from the nightmare we are facing.

Not surprising, the findings of her research are in keeping with what we eventually find out by experience. She wrote *"Bargaining rarely provides a sustainable solution especially if it's a matter of life and death."*

My sentiments exactly. I had a rude awakening when every attempt to *patch up* my relationship with my husband eventually failed. In fact, I now liken this *patchwork* mentality to the story of Adam and Eve. Remember, they sewed fig leaves to try and clothe themselves after eating the apple. What they were trying to do was cover their sense of guilt and shame.

Similarly, couples in an abusive relationship often make fig-leaf deals with each other for a while. We promise to change before reverting back to the same old habits sooner or later. We even try our best to be totally subservient and do anything to please our man. But none of these methods work for long.

There is no way around it. We must face it. The only way for our relationships to experience lasting change is that *we* must change. Upon reflection, I can now see the root cause of our dysfunctional behaviour as a couple is traceable to foundational issues such as esteem, respect and incompatible core values.

The construction industry has shown that the depth of the foundation basically determines the height and strength of the building. Men do not build sky scrapers on ten inch thick foundations. That would be ludicrous. Making buildings strong and safe is not a one-size-fits-all affair. On the contrary, varying formulation and materials are used to construct different types of foundation depending on the desired size, height, purpose and location of the building.

Furthermore, if the foundation is damaged in any way, it cannot simply be patched up. It must be repaired and fortified which is usually costly and time consuming. If proper corrective action, is not taken, the entire building is in danger of collapse – and to all intents of purposes – that building is condemned.

Screening your relationship in this light may help you correctly diagnose some of the foundational causes of domestic violence in your home. Try and identify as many causes as possible since this will give you wisdom and help you take ownership of the solution.

Ask yourself what has your marriage had to withstand? What pressures act as a catalyst to violent outbursts? Are there any outside influences which contribute to the abuse? What was your relationship based on from its conception?

The answers are as varied as there are people but common ailments give rise to domestic violence such as:

- A controlling spouse
- Alcohol or drug abuse
- Debt and financial worries
- Pregnancy and Childbirth
- Jealousy and possessiveness
- Cultural expectations of women
- Witnessing abuse as a child
- Incompatible core values
- Low Esteem
- Obsessively selfish desires

Once you can identify the factors influencing your situation you have placed yourself at an advantage.

This is because, instead of bargaining from a perceived position of helplessness and weakness, you begin to confront the issue from the position of clarity and choice. This perspective helps to eliminate a victim mentality which we are all prone to suffering from under the circumstances. It helps you to redevelop the confidence to communicate your expectations and need for respect.

Taking ownership of the mess you find yourself in really does give you so much more clarity about the whole situation. You begin to crystallise in your own mind, what you want and what you are no longer willing to accept.

You weigh up the answers to questions such as: What sort of relationship do I really want? What are the values I choose to live by? What is important to me now? What am I willing to accept? What won't I tolerate? Basically you start to rebuild a mental picture of the relationship you actually desire.

Whether you manage to redeem your marriage or your relationship fails, it is always wise to carry out this assessment. You need to know, what went wrong and what you would do differently, given the chance. Make the paradigm shift and engage in the process of change. The benefits far outweigh any discomfort you may feel. This process will make you more astute and the wisdom you gain will help to steer your relationship decisions in future.

Make no mistake. You can only be responsible for changing yourself and your own outlook. Your husband or partner must make up their own minds. But don't wait for him, start anyway.

Overcoming negative emotions and mindsets and instilling in their place positive expectations takes time. It takes a personal commitment to your future. If you know you never want to go though domestic abuse again, then this process is essential.

This is what happened to me. These are the questions I concerned myself with after I had regained my emotional equilibrium and was looking ahead to the future. I began to understand that the solution I was seeking couldn't just happen. To be honest, it has become clearer to me now why some people divorce and others don't. If only one person in the relationship decides to make the change and the other insists on remaining the same, there is a slim chance of happiness for that couple.

Having said that, in many cases, a change in you will elicit a change in them. What we are talking about takes time. Months, if not years. It is important to take the long term view. I believe that both you and your husband must be given time to work through these decisions before an end is put to the marriage.

You may ask why then did my marriage end?. I can only be honest and share with you; having done all; there are always cases where, the decision to end the marriage is taken out of your hands. We had two good chances over fourteen years to get it right. But in the end, habitual abuse coupled with deceit and betrayal took its toll. The wages of sin are indeed death – albeit death of a marriage. Be warned, if there is not a drastic change in behaviour and attitude, your relationship will die. Oppression has a price. Sustained domestic abuse has a price. Once intimacy, respect and trust fail, the marriage inevitably follows.

I know of instances where one of the couple gets a new partner or starts a new family during the time of separation. In these cases also, divorce is more likely. Yet I still believe you have not lost out if you have upheld your integrity throughout the whole painful and messy process. Take heart when it all falls apart. Trust that the lessons you have learned and the wisdom you have gained will serve you well in the future.

Today I am in the fortunate position of having made those decisions and I am much happier for it. I am very clear on what constitutes my non-negotiables. These are attributes you want your next partner to have so that you develop a healthy relationship. For instance, I value kindness and friendship above status or money among other things. The question is, what are you non-negotiables? Take time to think yours through and write them down.

Whatever your circumstances, it is not too late. I made many mistakes as I'm sure you have too. But the beauty of still having life is that we have been given another chance to get it right.

In a nutshell, don't get caught up in the fruitless

exercise of bargaining away your standards, values and respect. It is far more profitable to focus on permanently fixing the problem.

Depression

The word *depression* conjures up images of a person hopelessly lost in a deep melancholy, sadness or emotional low state over a long period of time. The compact oxford dictionary defines depression as *'severe despondency and dejection, especially when long-lasting and accompanied by physical symptoms'*

In actuality, depression and its symptoms may vary from feeling a little low in spirit and lethargic for a few days to constantly living in a deep pit of despair as described above.

Some people are suffering from deep clinical depression which will require professional medical diagnosis and intervention.

But there are other forms of depression, though not as severe, they feel just as real. When you are recovering from an abusive relationship, you will have days when you feel emotionally low. I think this is inescapable. Symptoms include, becoming complacent about your appearance and life in general. Nothing much makes sense anymore and you simply exist. No major plans. No real goals or dreams. It is as if, life has been snuffed out of you. Your *joie de vivre* has been quenched.

Funnily enough, possessing a happy or sunny personality doesn't seem to inoculate you from this season either. If you asked those who know me, they would describe me as a naturally effervescent and optimistic person – yet depression was certainly part of my experience

I remember that the slightest thing could trigger a tearful response. Days would pass without much focus or achievement only meditation and contemplation on what had just happened. Having tried every avenue to bargain with my husband, all to no avail – I felt trapped and this only fueled my depression.

On a positive note, watching my beautiful daughters grow up was the one saving grace of this period. They were and still are a constant source of happiness and laughter. Yet even that was blighted initially by my deep sadness over the fact that I wasn't able to provide the standard of living for them that I had always dreamed of.

In a way it's like grieving over a lost person except we grieve over lost relationships, a broken ideal, what could have been. I am writing this book to encourage those of you who are going through this that rest assured; you will come out of it. I refer you back to previous chapter where I touched on things you can do to overcome the loneliness. Building friendships, learning new skills and volunteering may not lessen the pain but they help to turn your focus away from the endless hours of analysis and self accusations.

One of the best medicines I have found to treat depression is to involve yourself in helping others. Somehow, being a blessing and source of encouragement to others is both cathartic and it has a surprising way of making you feel good. Plus it keeps you busy.

One day, perhaps after weeks, but more likely after months have passed, you will finally come to the place of acceptance

Acceptance

In my case, the day of acceptance is clearly defined. For you, it may be a series of events. One day while standing by the kitchen sink, thoughts to this effect, came to my mind:

'Vivien, this is it for now. It's not fair, nor is it right but you can build from here. Thank God, you have your strength and your life with two beautiful daughters to show for it. Now roll up your sleeves and get to work.'

The state of acceptance is not passive at all. Rather it involves acknowledging what you have suffered and resolving not to let it keep you down or knock you out of the game of life. It is taking back control of your life and refusing to remain a victim. It is deciding in the face of adversity to move on regardless. It is looking in the mirror and saying to yourself the words so famously coined by the US President, Barak Obama during his 2012 re-election campaign – *"Forward"*.

In conclusion, the road to recovery for all sufferers of domestic violence may seem long, protracted and loaded with many painful memories. But with persistence, commitment and time, there is an end in sight. A good end. Every stage has its benefits and there are lessons you can glean from each one. Since you have been compelled to travel down this road, you may as well make it work for you. I hope the ideas posed in this chapter will be useful to you in making your journey of recovery that much easier than mine.

It is time to turn the page. At this juncture, I feel the need to point to a large warning sign ahead – *Watch out for the Potholes.*

CHAPTER 9

Watch Out for the Potholes

Any road that falls into disrepair develops potholes. Large deep holes or dents in the road which could damage the wheels of your car if care is not taken to avoid them. At best, potholes can cause suspension and steering problems. At worst, driving full speed into a pothole could wreck your car entirely and bring your journey to an abrupt halt.

Such are the repercussions of these two relationship mistakes, made by people recovering from abusive relationships.

The first one is what I call *Rebound Relationships* with another man.

The second one is *Premature Reconciliation* with your husband or partner.

There is a third scenario reserved for special cases where I advise *Zero Contact*.

Rebound Relationships

I have included this section so it may act as a word of caution to all you ladies who are convinced that the reason for your suffering is all the man's fault. He may have been the aggressor and physically to blame. However, as we have discussed in previous chapters, we as women must also squarely confront the role we had to play in the breakdown of our relationships. This in my opinion is the best safeguard against making the same mistakes all over again.

If you have a litter of two or more violent or abusive relationships behind you, then please please listen to what I am saying. Many times, women fall into the same trap over and over again and even marry partners of similar disposition but under different circumstances. That is why I believe that the process of giving yourself time is essential to the success of your future relationships.

Only with time can you hope to fully:
- Recover from domestic violence
- Assess key factors
- Strengthen your esteem
- Develop confidence in your core values

Personally speaking, when we first separated, I wasn't at all interested in men, especially since I was still married. But in any case, I viewed all men with suspicion for a while. After my divorce, I was so disheartened with marriage that I swung to the other extreme. I wanted to be in relationship with a man but not hiiiim! But I was put off marriage completely. As a woman of faith, this was problematic since I knew what the scriptures had to stay about co-habiting with someone. Thankfully I didn't give in to temptation which was ever present trust me. Now I am at the point where I truly believe, I will marry again to the right person, at the right time.

When your break up is still fresh, part of you begins to miss your other half. You are used to being part of a couple and having someone there to share things with – good and bad.

One of the unforeseen consequences of being single again is that you can get lonely. Furthermore, celibacy is now forced upon you. Need I say more?? Then thirdly if you are a single parent you suddenly become Mummy, Daddy, Breadwinner and Nurturer all in one! A weighty burden indeed.

This craving for adult company can lead you to start a new relationship with a man prematurely. It is a real trap which can only be avoided by making a quality decision upfront. In my view, judging by what I went through and what others I know have experienced, nothing short staying single for a year or two can be sufficient.

What?! I can sense your shock already. I didn't exactly plan it that way but I definitely saw the sense in it after I had lived through it plus I have discussed this issue with other women in similar circumstances and the majority agrees.

During this time, there is no need to sit home twiddling your thumbs, watching romance flicks! To be fair, there is no hard and fast rule to this. *But* it is wise to seek out your own company and friends to whom you are wiling to become accountable. Otherwise – I warn you now – you may find it becomes very easy to throw caution and reason to the wind against your better judgment. After all, it is a well known fact that we women are more emotional than men and our primary objective is to make the best choice possible next time round – not repeat past mistakes.

Another reason why you may consider waiting a while concerns the much studied phenomena of *attraction*. Somehow, unless we heal and become whole, we tend to subliminally attract the same type of men into our lives and the cycle continues.

Let's face it; most relationships are sweet at the beginning. Imagine the scenario for a moment. You meet another man whom you really like. He is so kind and caring. You get to know one another. He is even compassionate about what you've suffered in the past. At first he seems a world away from the brute beast you left behind. Right?

You let your guard down, fall in love and everyone is happy. He seems a little possessive but hey, that's chicken feed compared to what you were subjected to in your previous relationship. You can handle it. Now your heart is taken, any obvious signs of brewing trouble are quickly dispelled, justified or shoved to the back of your brain. Can you see how easily we persuade ourselves that this guy is different; forgetting that our previous partner was just as attentive at the beginning as well.

Then, for whatever reason, those tell tale signs you initially ignored start interrupting your revelry and soon become roaring realities. Before you know it, another cycle of violence and abuse begins and you find yourself in a living nightmare once again.

I realize that this is a simple summation of an often complex process of learning to trust and love again. Yet the point I am trying to make is that when you have not given yourself enough time to become a whole person, you run a very high risk of making bad relationship decisions and falling into this pothole on the rebound.

How many women have hastily changed partners, only to realize they had jumped from the frying pan into the fire? Worse still, if you have children, there is an additional risk that your new partner will also become abusive to your children.

The temptation to rush may be heightened if your ex gets someone else in his life. Argh! Now you want to go on a mission to prove to him you can do it too. I admit these feelings may be natural. But I must also point out that giving in to them could lead to more misery later if not well thought out.

I hope this doesn't sound too pessimistic since my intention is not to instill fear but rather to stress the importance of you not rushing into a relationship driven by loneliness, frustration or even revenge

I believe any real danger we face in regards to our vulnerability to this pothole can be overcome if we just tread carefully, check our emotions and prayerfully seek God's counsel and feedback from people who really know us and love us. Introduce your new beau to them and take the opportunity to meet his friends as well. Then ask for their opinion. Don't be too defensive and secretive about your relationship because at the end of the day, it is better to be safe than sorry.

Premature Reconciliation

This is the second pothole which I have already alluded to. In fact, in some ways, this presents a greater temptation than the former one. Only because it may feel easier to slip back into a relationship with someone you already know than building a new one. Ever heard the phrase *'better the devil you know, than the devil you don't'?*

Reconciliation is a worthy goal if both of you commit to making the necessary changes. First time round, my husband and I got back on speaking terms after some months for the sake of our daughter. He used to visit her often and in so doing we would see each other regularly. However, this did not mean that we were ready to reconcile right away.

Both of you need to work through your individual and joint issues and openly discuss the changes you expect from each other. Skipping or eliminating this step before reconciliation can be compared to a wound not healing properly after an operation. There is a high risk of infection setting in.

Again you may find yourself missing their company or during one of the times he visits the kids that old attraction may spring up. This is why I am a great supporter of premeditated thought and decision making.

Just as ladies can make a quality decision *not* to rush into any new relationship on the rebound, you can decide which areas you need to see deep changes in your husband or partner before you are willing to consider reconciling with him. Some reconcile before divorce as was my case, others may reconcile after divorce. But the conditions required remain the same.

Ask yourself, has he repented? By this I am not asking, has he merely apologised? I mean, has he admitted to himself, you and others that he has a problem with anger and violence and sought to get help or make a change. Believe me if he hasn't, it will be all too easy for him to fall back into the same old habits. Only a change of heart and mind can induce permanent change.

This step may sound simple but it is usually the most difficult and could take months, sometimes years. You see, as long as he feels that expressing his anger towards you in a violent fashion is acceptable, then it remains difficult for him to stop.

The fact of the matter is, he is *capable* of stopping. If he wasn't he would display the same behaviour towards others people like his sister, co-worker or friend. But this is usually not the case is it? So the question becomes, is he *willing* to change his pattern of behaviour towards *you?*

Many times, women say things like '*I still love him*' or because they are still physically attracted to him, they feel this is a good premise for reconciliation.

No – a thousand times – No! Ultimately, whether

you still love him or find him attractive is the least consideration. You must address the underlying factors of domestic abuse and make the necessary changes before you can even hope to break the cycle. It will take one set of skills and principles to break the abuse. Then another set of skills and practices entirely to rebuild a successful relationship. That is why a permanent change of heart, and attitude is paramount for both parties. This does not happen overnight. It comes as a result of sustained renewal of mind, engineered by the word of God within an arena of accountability.

We have already discussed what you need to do. But how can you identify changes in him?

You can perceive a change of heart simply by observing his words and behaviour when he is with you. I found that at the beginning it wouldn't take long before my husband would accuse me of something or other. This was a big clue that he still held me solely responsible for our separation. Abusive, critical or sarcastic language are all red lights to any thoughts of reconciliation.

Another key indicator is how he respects your time. How does he approach you when making appointments to come over and see the children? Is he demanding? Does he request to know when you are available or does he assume he can turn up whenever he wants. Also, does he always demand or expect things to be done on his terms? Or is he overly intrusive to know your movements on a daily basis? These types of controlling overtures should put you on the alert *against* reconciliation.

Let me touch on a frequent tactic many men use. They *purposely* try and seduce you back into bed with them. It happens all the time. Oldest trick in the book but too many women fall for it! Men use this tactic because they know that once you receive them back sexually it will be much easier to break down your defenses. They will try and sweet talk you and tell you how much they miss you which may be true. However, dear lady, there is a process to reconciliation. Jumping into bed may feel good today but will it prevent abuse tomorrow? You must do more to investigate whether this is merely a surface change of heart or does it go deeper than that – namely is there any evidence of accountability, acceptance and change.

It is easy to safeguard yourself against sexual advances by ensuring you meet up in public places. In fact I continued to meet my husband in public places for some years until I was confident of his sincerity towards making changes. Meeting in public also helped us to maintain cordial communication.

Do all you can to maintain a civil and respectful

rapport with one another, especially if you have children. I do not advise making negative comments about their Daddy to your children. Children, on the whole, want to love their Daddies and seem to weather the whole ordeal of parental separation much better if they enjoy regular contact with their father.

Believe me, trying to rebuild bridges with your husband or partner is not easy. It can be a difficult balancing act and learning curve. On the one hand, you want the father of your children to maintain contact with them as much as possible. On the other hand, you do not wish to tolerate abusive or degrading behaviour from him in any way.

Now certain actions and words should become off limits. Personally I show no tolerance towards anyone, especially men who begin to profusely swear or use derogatory language when they are talking to me. You must set your own boundaries and stick to them. All this is part of the psychological training you are putting yourself through before moving onto another relationship or reconciling with your ex.

There were times when I literally had to cut visits short because the conversation became particularly nasty or rude. I would excuse myself, pack up our daughter and leave. Here is another reason why meeting in public places is so beneficial! It allows you the scope to leave when necessary. If you meet up in your house it is far more difficult to get him to go without it getting nasty. You know the buttons that set you off and so does he. Once tempers get heated, another nasty episode may ensue. So prevention is definitely better than cure.

Try this for yourself and watch the outcome. If you discipline yourself to do this once or twice, he will receive the message loud and clear that you are serious and mean business. Hopefully, from then on, you will observe some improvement as he tries to avoid making similar mistakes in your future meetings. Then gradually your communication will improve.

Don't be discouraged if things initially get out of hand more than once All the steps I have mentioned above took us a long while to achieve. The process may be painfully slow but when you persevere you will reap the rewards of rebuilding healthy communication boundaries between the two of you.

These steps helped me to restore cordial communication with my ex husband and it is an ongoing process up until today. The lessons I have learnt are invaluable and I hope they will assist you to reopen the channels of healthy communication. If there are no kids involved, then this is not as essential.

Over the years, I have known women on both sides of the equation: namely, those who waited and those who rushed. The end result always seems to be better if we wait.

Zero Contact

People think that separation or divorce marks the end of the matter. This is not always the case. In some extreme cases the controlling nature of the abusive men has taken hold to such a degree that it drives them to seek revenge at any cost. They attempt to torture their ex-wives emotionally, verbally and legally for years.

Men have been known to instigate hate campaigns in the press or media against their spouse. They bring incriminating trumped up charges against them. They try and distance the children from their mother and concoct slanderous reports. The lengths they go to is absolutely incredible. In such cases, the only thing a woman can do is keep her poise, live her life and focus on her future. There is no point in maintaining contact beyond that which is *absolutely* necessary.

When a man possesses such a toxic attitude, they are prone to using every known detail of your life against you. Words are twisted. Events are fabricated and their own actions are hidden or defended. Basically they try and wear you down and scatter your focus. Responding to each infraction may prove to be a waste of time and money.

> *"Never waste your time trying to explain who you are to people who are committed to misunderstanding you." (anon)*

After all has been said and done; how many court cases can you attend or how many accusations can you defend? Hard as it may seem, you must determine to rise above the intimidation and furtive tactics. You may even have to move away. Especially when it seems your abusive ex is not content until he literally destroys you. My advice is: Ignore him as much as you can and go on about your business. However the sad reality is, a part of you must remain on guard. So be careful. Be prayerful. Be circumspect and be watchful.

CHAPTER 10

For Bitter or For Better?

Many times we are prone to thinking that forgiveness is a feeling, yet it is primarily a choice. It is only human to feel a sense of injustice when you have been maltreated. But this sense leads most of us to want to retaliate against the culprit who hurt us or abused us. This may involve inflicting pain or some other worse fate on him or her. Anything that makes us feel they have suffered to *at least the same* degree that we have at their own hands.

This chapter will help you tackle the bitterness you feel against your husband or partner and also, we will discuss how you can forgive and heal from grief brought on by the abuse in your home.

If the whole ordeal of domestic violence is still going on as you read this book, be warned that the longer you permit your spouse to continue their aggression, the more risk you are taking of exposing yourself to intense feelings of anger, bitterness and revenge. Feelings which if bottled up may eventually spill over into a vicious attack or self defence, causing you to harm them.

So I am taking a moment to re-emphasise two points:

1) You should seek help now or risk being pushed to a dangerous point.

Hopefully I have reinforced this idea throughout the book and the message has hit home loud and clear. In the introduction I made a statement; *'there is hope for you and your family but the catch is, you must save your life before you can save your home'*. Precisely.

2) Decide to forgive, or at least be willing to tackle the process of forgiveness.

I clearly remember the feelings of injustice and anger. It used to rise like bile in my throat at odd times anytime I would think about what happened. What upset me most – wasn't just the violence itself – but all the insults and lies that were spread about me and his complete betrayal – making me feel like this marriage had literally brought me to nothing. I was made to feel like a rag doll.

Many times I would break down in tears or cry out to God and ask that all-encompassing question *'Why?!'* In the early days, there were very few people I told what was going on. But even when I did finally open up, much of what they had to offer was accusing questions and empty platitudes. Typical questions like "what did you do to make him angry?" The quick answer was, sometimes nothing, sometimes an argument, but as far as I was concerned, what difference did it make?! If everyone who got upset lashed out in violence, what would the world come to?

Other people would offer platitudes such as *'keep praying'* – *'God will do it'* – *'Just submit, and he will calm down'*. Unbelievably one elderly lady told me, as far as she was concerned, domestic violence was not all that unusual. She went on further to say that, in her day, it happened all the time and prided herself on the fact that she *never* called the police. What was her overall advice? I should just pray and bear it. I was shocked at the level of complacency, ignorance and acceptance I encountered, especially among believers!

Christians who were born again, spirit filled followers of Christ and yet they didn't seem to have any answers. Make no mistake, I in no way blame the church for what happened. I am a fervent believer who still attends and enjoys church but my heartfelt desire is that we Christians would open our eyes and ears a little more to what is going on out there and get involved in lifting hurting people out of domestic abuse. Real concern is not passive.

No one was bold enough to confront my husband for years. All the advice seemed to centre on what I should do or what I was not doing. I took it on board and did everything in my power but after years of trying to improve and perfect being a "dutiful" wife, the abuse continued. This confused me at first when I was still young in faith. However when I took all my angst directly to the Lord in prayer and asked him what is going on, He clearly gave me the wisdom and grace to tackle the situation through His word.

I really empathise with women who hold deeply rooted beliefs and moral principles because it often feels like you are walking a knife edge. On the one hand, you want to honour your upbringing and culture or principles of faith. Whereas, on the other hand, you are in real and present danger. The jeopardy for many women is, in trying to uphold our principles and beliefs, we tolerate the untenable for such a long time, that we are eaten alive by bitterness and hatred.

I knew the bitterness was hurting me, because my persona changed and I knew that forgiving was the right thing to do. Yet somehow, despite the fact I am the type of person who normally finds it draining to hold a grudge for very long, forgiving my ex husband was especially hard.

Paradoxically, when we were still married, it was easier for me to release him after each episode. I dealt with feelings of anger and bitterness on a daily basis by worshipping in the bathroom and then releasing him. As things worsened, it took longer for us to start talking again but I maintained this habit of releasing him daily. That is how I managed to enjoy the good days in between the bad ones.

The main hindrance I faced in trying to forgive my ex-husband was I had to work through the issue of justice. Because the wounds ran so deep and the pain I felt in my heart was palpable at times. There is definitely such a thing as heart break. It's not just an expression. It is a physical condition which is nothing short of agonising. The pain was compounded by watching my children suffer as well. Their lives were disrupted by us having to move house and find new schools and their hearts were broken by dashed hopes and disappointments. The weight of all that grief was overwhelming.

I fought as much for them as I did for our marriage. During all the years of our marriage, I held onto the belief that we could get past the abuse and have a good relationship. What I dearly wanted was a settled home. So when things finally deteriorated beyond repair and we did divorce, I felt like, it was a waste of fourteen years. Especially the last four years. I just felt like it was pointless and I should have saved myself the heartache and walked away the first time. So many regrets overwhelmed me. My pre-eminent question became *'where was the justice if I forgave him?'* How *could he take so many years of my life, misuse them, betray my trust and support and literally cause my children and I to be brought to nothing, culminating in us loosing our home and then walk away without paying for his deeds?'*

Yet in my heart of hearts, I knew the bitterness and bile in my throat had to go. Though I was glad to finally get away, I definitely needed special grace to forgive him for all he had put the children and me through.

It is important you choose to forgive, not primarily for the benefit of the person who hurt you but for your own sake. Forgiveness marks the start of your emotional healing. Moving on without forgiveness will hamper your well being and affect every future relationship you have.

Therefore I strongly encourage you to make the choice to forgive, no matter how hard it may be. We make the quality decision but the strength and grace to carry it through comes from God. The saying goes *'to err is human, to forgive is divine'*. I could not agree more.

Thankfully, I did find that special grace, hidden in one scripture and one spiritual practice. The combined effect of these things enabled me to finally forgive my ex-husband and his family, whom I felt were silent accomplices in the whole affair. The scripture said;

> **Romans 12:19** *Beloved do not avenge yourselves, but give place to wrath; for it is written Vengeance is Mine, I will repay" says the Lord.*

By this word I took away four spiritual principles which undergird the issues of forgiveness;

- It is not our rightful place to retaliate or mete out justice.
- The Lord assumes ultimate responsibility for judgement between people.
- God recognises there has been a breach of justice and *will bring recompense.* This is so true. Years down the road, I have seen evidence of this as He has faithfully orchestrated events in my life to compensate my children and I for our felt suffering and loss.
- Finally God is the prosecutor and the defence plus He acts as both Judge and Jury over the matter, so He will execute fitting justice on your behalf.

The wisdom of this spiritual advice is so aptly demonstrated by our police and government. Any civilised society actively discourages vigilante acts or *jungle justice* as we call it in Africa. When a crime has been committed, we are not supposed to take the law into our own hands. The correct thing for the aggrieved party to do is to seek justice by following the proper recourse through the courts according to the law.

Once I fully grasped this concept and trusted that justice would eventually be served, I no longer felt the need for my ex husband to give *me his pound of flesh*. The reality is, he couldn't repay me anyway and neither can your spouse. When our sense of injustice is heightened, we keep thinking, he cannot just get away with it! Surely he must pay for what he did. Well yes, our accounts do need to be settled but not by the person who committed the offence.

Think about it this way. Your husband or partner could never give you back what you lost. Even if he was to try and make it up to you, he could only apologise and take steps to stop the abuse, but it is not within his human power to "refund" the days, hours, and years you lost. Nor can he compensate you for all your blood, sweat and tears. That domain belongs solely to God who gives life. Jesus shed His blood on the cross to pay for every deficit and illegal act. So He *can restore the years* that have been lost and He is able to heal the pain, if only you will trust Him.

Healing from Grief

People say time will heal and in my opinion this is only partly true. Grief involves sorrow but it is much deeper than that. Grief involves mourning, yet it is more than that too. Grief comes from our spirit; that deep place where no man can touch and nothing on earth can heal. Grief can overwhelm you two days or two years after the event. It is very unpredictable. You can be fine one minute and suddenly plunged into grief the next minute due to a trigger such as a place, a song or flashback.

So what hope is there for those who grieve? Well, I discovered that the only real antidote of grief is *Joy*. Joy heals, restores and rejuvenates our soul plus Joy brings back a sense of pleasure into our being. I can hear you asking – tell me quickly please – how can I get my joy back? For the record, here are four great ways. Hopefully these suggestions will help you.

Firstly, you should identify the people who make you happy and spend time with them. For instance, just watching the goofy things my children do brings me joy. We have spent countless hours together just laughing, playing music, dancing and eating. They really have been my saving grace.

Secondly find a place of beauty or awe and drink it in. This sounds simple enough but it makes a massive difference. If you have no money, pack a picnic and go to the park or the beach! If you have to relocate, move to the best area you can. Just being in nice surroundings alone can buoy up your spirits.

Then thirdly; invest your time and energy into pursuing what you enjoy or are passionate about. My three loves are working in ministry, running my charity and doing up property. I remember when my firstborn was still in nappies, my friend and I used to strap our kids into their buggies and visit property exhibitions because we both loved houses. This was such an uplifting way of building our dreams.

Last but by no means least; you will find joy in God's Presence. This is the spiritual practice I was referring to earlier. Simply worship. Find a place, a group or a CD where people are in sincere worship to Jesus and join in. Overdose on God's presence. Let a part of heaven invade your being here on earth and you will experience *lasting healing* from your grief.

> ***Psalm 16:11*** *"In His Presence is fullness of Joy and at His right hand, pleasures for ever more."*

The fruits of doing all the above are: today I am

free, physically, mentally and emotionally. I am very happy and my renewed vigour for life keeps increasing. No matter how difficult it may seem, I hope you will also choose to forgive because forgiveness generates the power you need to transform *the bitter into better.*

CHAPTER 11

The Three Stages to Forgiveness

Fundamentally, forgiving your husband or partner is going to be an act of your will by choice not an emotional decision. We have acknowledged the difficulties and now I want to share a little about the rewards and dividends you shall receive when you do forgive.

There are essentially three stages to forgiveness which are:

Stage One You must decide to forgive which in essence means being willing to let it go.

A wise person once said, "Unforgiveness is like drinking someone else's poison and expecting them to die". It just doesn't work that way does it? Forgiveness means you choose to release that person from the debt they owe you. In truth, domestic abuse can be counted as an IOU.

Don't be alarmed when you forgive, if you do not feel an immediate sense of relief from the pain. You will definitely walk in a greater *sense of peace*. From this point onwards, your healing can truly begin. How much would you pay to be free enough to live again and love again? Unfortunately money is not able to buy back your peace of mind in this case. Still, life is challenging enough without being weighed down by the extra baggage of bitterness and resentment.

Stage Two Even though you have determined to forgive, you must continually seek the grace to forgive. It does not usually come automatically. The grace I needed came through healing from grief, reading scripture and flooding my being with the presence of God by listening to gospel music and worshipping.

Practically speaking, it does not help to replay scenes from the past through your mind like a silent movie. Avoid insulting your husband to your children. There are benefits to expressing and verbalising your experiences to trusted confidantes. However, I do not advise continuing for years to rehash events over and over. Talking about it incessantly is counterproductive since it disturbs your peace of mind and opens up old sores and wounds

The time will come when you will be able to recount events, without pain. That is when you will *know* that you have recovered. By that time, your life will have moved on to such an extent, you that you have actually forgotten certain scenes and no longer wish to recall them.

Stage Three This is the final stage of release when you can be certain of the fact that you have truly forgiven. When you get to the place emotionally where you are able to wish your ex-husband or partner well and bless them, then the process of forgiveness is officially complete! One day in the future – hopefully sooner rather than later – this will happen to you.

So many atrocities have been committed by humanity but the power to capitalise on the evil actions people perpetrate has never come from retaliation.

Historically there are two well known men who demonstrated this virtue. They are Nelson Mandela from South Africa and Mahatma Ghandi from India. Both men led their nations to liberty from racially oppressive regimes and both men set an example of actively seeking the good of their fellow man *including* those who had beaten, tortured and opposed their cause.

Jesus taught on this aspect of forgiveness by instructing us to

Matthew 5:44 "*Love your enemies; bless*

> *those who curse you; do good to those who hate you and pray for those who spitefully use you and persecute you."*

This is a tall order indeed, yet highly rewarding once we are able to follow His advice.

Let me tell you what happens when we do this. When we actively pray for the person who hurt us, petitioning heaven for their good and show them mercy in our attitude and behaviour, a miracle happens.

You will actually begin to feel a sense of compassion for that person and you will want to see them healed and delivered, rather than suffering the consequences.

The only way I can describe this phenomena is that you will feel like a concerned sister or friend who sees the road someone is on and knows they are headed for trouble but wishes they would follow another road with better prospects.

I never felt like I wanted to marry my ex husband again but I definitely came to the place where I genuinely wished him well without any altruistic reasons of personal gain. What I am relaying to you is the miraculous testimony of how the Spirit of God can work in our hearts and life. I went from being an aggrieved, angry and emotionally battered woman to becoming a person able to offer him mercy, without rancour or bitterness. This state of liberty awaits you also if you will make the trip down the road of forgiveness.

Without a doubt, these three stages work if you work them. *As the love of God works through you, it will simultaneously heal you.* This is how it works. Forgiveness is very much like an onion. There are layers to the entire process. Sometimes, you may need to go back and repeat a stage when you are confronted with a particularly painful memory or event. That is ok, just keep doing it.

Forgive Yourself

One last discourse on this issue surrounds forgiving yourself. Nobody is perfect, but many women are wracked with guilt over how they handled their relationships. Others feel guilty for having gotten a divorce or for matters concerning the children. I am encouraging you to forgive yourself. Don't be so hard on yourself. Just because you failed to make it right, doesn't define YOU as a failure.

Harbouring un-forgiveness is a dangerous resistor to the flow of God's power in your life at the best of times. But the situation is made even worse when you condemn yourself because you run away from Him, not to Him.

The above stages are exactly the same for those who need to forgive themselves, but with one major difference: you are the donor *and* the recipient of the act of forgiveness. The truth is, you are already forgiven. Nothing is hidden from the eyes of the Lord. He knows all about your failures but His stance towards you remains unchanged. He has already taken care of the penalties involved for every misdemeanour, failure, error and shortcoming by sending His own sinless son – Jesus – to the cross to make eternal payment. So your debt has been paid in full! Jesus has paid for it for you.

With this in mind, you can see that the *guilt and condemnation* you are feeling doesn't come from the Lord. People may try and load it back upon you but God's heart towards you is mercy and even now, His hand is stretched out towards you, offering you unconditional love, acceptance and forgiveness. Totally, without reservation or hesitation.

All you have to do is pray and ask for it, then believe and accept it. The grace you need is freely available as a gift because Jesus already bore the full brunt of your guilt and shame on the cross. Consequently you and I no longer have to. The most profitable thing you can do for yourself is: take the decisive step to off load all those pent up feelings of guilt onto Jesus Receive His mercy and forgive yourself.

My final word on this topic is, you *deserve* to enjoy the liberation and peace of mind that only comes when you forgive yourself, forgive your husband or partner and… Set yourself free!

CHAPTER 12

Conclusion

Wherever you are in your struggle against domestic violence, I hope this book has provided you with the winning solutions and spiritual fortitude you require, so that you are able to deal effectively with the issue of abuse destroying your home.

"Courage is not the absence of fear. It is acting in spite of it." (M.Twain)

As I said early on, my heart's desire is to see women, from every walk of life and cultural background find help and hope as they seek to free themselves from the cycle of abuse.

There is *no* simple solution, but the master key that unlocks your freedom is and will always be – to take *action*.

Throughout this book, I have shared my story and given you a glimpse into my affairs solely for the purpose of equipping you with information whilst instilling courage in your heart to fight and win your own battle.

Every woman is different and every home has varying dynamics but the principles I have outlined in this book have stood the test of time. Principles based on love, honour, respect, the value of life, accountability and responsibility.

If I have managed to survive and overcome the whole painful experience, you can too. I firmly believe this. In fact I would go further to say that, every woman who manages to escape and to recover and becomes a beacon of hope for somebody else. It's a chain reaction.

Concluding Words

Dear Reader, the battle lines have been drawn. You may not have asked for it, but now that you find yourself caught in the war zone of domestic violence and abuse, *fight to win!* Fight to save your life. Fight for the future of your children. Fight to restore peace to your home and fight for your liberty; physically, spiritually and emotionally.

I am earnestly praying for you. We may not have met, but I know you are out there. I pray that *"violence shall no longer be heard in your land, neither wasting nor destruction within your borders; I pray that one day in the near future, you shall call the walls of your home Salvation (peace and security) and your gates Praise. May God preserve you from all evil and deliver you from all destruction, in the Name of Jesus I pray. Amen" (taken from Isaiah 60:18)*

Above all, do not surrender.

Author Profile

Vivien Rose is a writer, social entrepreneur and ordained Minister living in London. A devoted mother of two children, Vivien divides her time between working her business, serving in ministry and raising support for her charity **IGNITE Benevolence Fund** which provides assistance to survivors of domestic violence, and runs projects which nurture the potential of children, young people and women living in the UK and Africa.

Her facebook blog *"Picking Up the Pieces"* is a recovery resource attracting thousands of subscribers from around the world with posts that are injected with wisdom, comfort and inspiration, helping people to "turn their pain to gain".

Getting in Touch by Email

ignitepublishinghouse@gmail.com
office@igbfund.org

www.ingramcontent.com/pod-product-compliance
Lightning Source LLC
Chambersburg PA
CBHW071704040426
42446CB00011B/1908